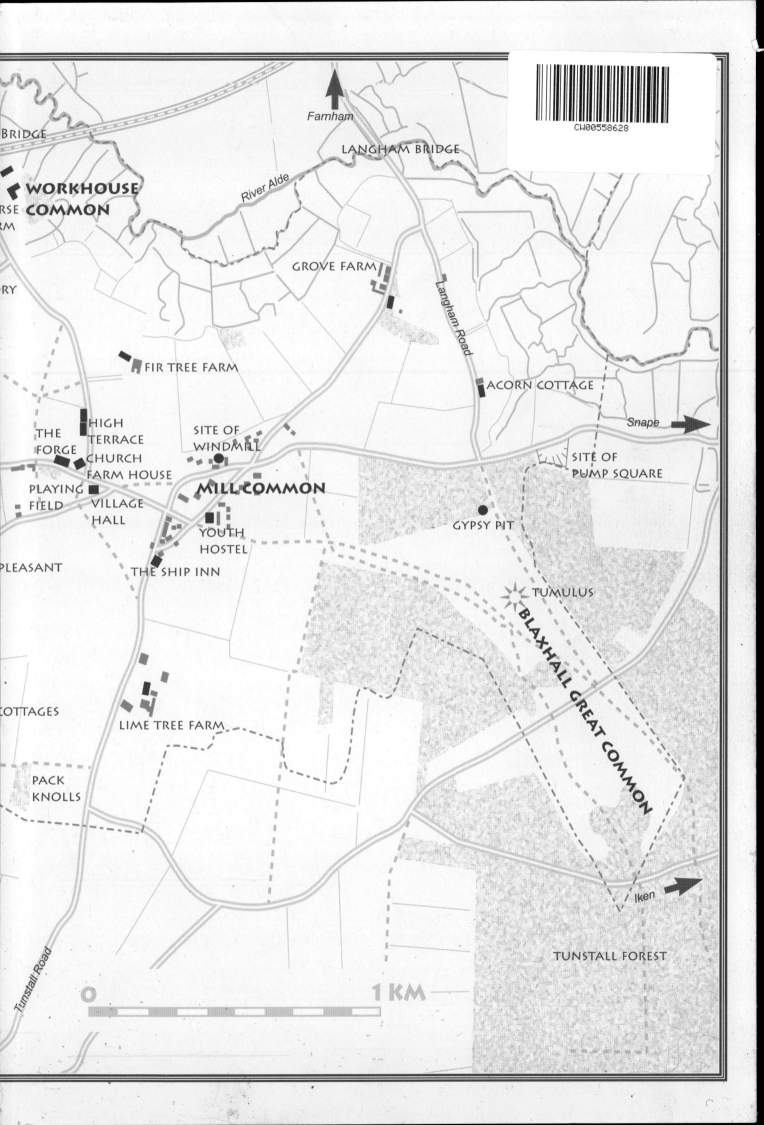

B L S T

S N A P F E

R

SI

D,

ENA PLANT, RAT POACHER, VIOLET SKEET, MARY SMITH, BERT SMITH

### FOREWORD
BY THE CHILDREN OF
FLORENCE AND GEORGE EWART EVANS

# DEDICATED TO
# BERT SMITH
# 1920 - 2006

George Smith with his master's sheep, Blaxhall, c.1910

# CONTENTS

First published in the United Kingdom in 2007
by the Blaxhall Archive Group, Blaxhall, Suffolk IP12 2DP

British Library Cataloguing in Publication Data
A catalogue record for this book is available from the British
Library

ISBN  978 0 9555389 0 2


Typeset in 11/14 Antigua
Design and layout: Blaxhall Archive Group
Printed by: The Lavenham Press, Lavenham, Suffolk

# FOREWORD

When our parents, Florence and George Ewart Evans, escaped post - war London to live in Blaxhall it is unlikely that they imagined that over half a century later their four children would be invited to contribute the Foreword to "Blaxhall's Living Past". It is a great credit to the archive group that the pioneering interest in oral history our father showed in the village and recorded initially in "Ask the Fellows who Cut the Hay" has been developed in such depth by the archive group. The Bygones exhibition in the Parish room and this excellent and comprehensive book serve to underline the importance of recording oral history.

It is rather sobering to realise that the eight happy and formative years we spent in the village are now part of living history and our experiences are shared with many still resident in Blaxhall. It is a pleasure to read their accounts of childhood and remember that we too picked blackberries for Mrs Taylor's shop on Stone Common, collected acorns for the Forestry Commission, roamed wild on the heath and watched at harvest time as the threshing machine closed in on the centre of the field flushing out the rabbits and hares sheltering there. This book brings such memories back to life.

**Mary Gerson (née Evans)**
**Susan Gentleman (née Evans)**
**Jane Palmer (née Evans)**
**Matthew Evans**

March 2007

# PREFACE AND ACKNOWLEDGEMENTS

The contents of this book are largely the result of on-going research, both in the field and in the archives by members of the Blaxhall Archive Group (BAG). As such it is a miscellany in words and pictures of particular periods and aspects of Blaxhall's story; it is not an attempt to relate an unbroken history but rather a random collection of 'snapshots of village life'.

The book's structure is dictated by our wish to capture these snapshots for future reference and interest in a format which allows us to share our information with all the present residents of the village.

The project would not have been possible without community support over the past four years, so we are greatly indebted to all those Blaxhallites both past and present, too numerous to name individually, who have contributed directly or indirectly through one way or another to its fruition. We are especially grateful to those who have given access and to those who have contributed family photographs. We would also like to thank the staff at the Ipswich branch of the Suffolk Records Office, especially Bridget Hanley and Jayne Austin for their invaluable help, advice and support.

Thanks also go to the people and institutions that have allowed us to use images of their documents and maps from their archives: in particular, Major Philip Hope-Cobbold for allowing us to use images from the North/Cobbold archive; and Suffolk County Council - Education Department for extracts from the Blaxhall School logbooks.

One of the highlights of this project has been to meet Reg and Ada Mannall and through them to be privileged to use some of the unique collection of photographs taken by their aunt Ada Mannall; we thank them wholeheartedly.

Finally, we must thank our sponsors without whom we would not have had the finance to complete this project. The Local Heritage Initiative is a national grant scheme that helps local groups to investigate, explain and care for our local landscape, landmarks, traditions and culture. The Heritage Lottery Fund (HLF) provides the grant but the scheme is a partnership, administered by the Countryside Agency with additional funding from Nationwide Building Society.

# INTRODUCTION

# THE TIME BEFORE THIS

A few memories from some of the Blaxhall Archive Group members

## Introduction by Maggie Grenham

In 1999 I found myself moving to Stone Common, Blaxhall, Suffolk and in the next few years I became aware of the village's uniqueness. My first insight of the village history was through the book *'Ask the Fellows who Cut the Hay'* by George Ewart Evans[1]. He had built up a unique picture of the village through his writing, film and oral history taping.

It was from a Bygones exhibition held in the village hall that I first had the thought that very soon we would be losing not only the older generation of Blaxhallites, but also the ability to be able to name and identify people and places that were recorded in these photographs.

My first exploration led me on a very tentative journey; I had been told that Kenny French known locally as "the Sheriff" had a collection of photographs and slides.

It was to be a few more years before I plucked up enough courage to ask Kenny about the photographs. So one day after the floods of 2001 when Kenny was standing outside his house we got talking and I thought if I don't ask him now it's going to be too late.

So I said I'd bring a bottle around and if possible could I see all these photographs – to which he replied "don't do that I have a bottle that I was saving for my wedding and I think that it might end up being used at my funeral". Sadly I had been too late as within days Kenny had become ill and was never to return to the village. So what was I to do now?

It was then that I started to chat to Ray Poacher and with his help I started to be able to meet locals who would end up loaning photographs that we could scan and save. The two of us grew eventually into 15 and our meetings of BAG became regular meetings on a Tuesday when we looked at photographs and began annotating them.

After a number of months it became clear that we would be in charge of an amazing photographic collection with many stories.

So it was from here that the idea came about that the Blaxhall Archive Group could possibly produce a book and maybe a DVD. And so after a journey of nearly seven years we are finally here with a grant from LHI to publish the collection.

It was during 2005 and prior to our exhibition called Blaxhall's Living Past that members of the group put together a piece of text which we turned into a poster. It has now developed into the short introduction you are about to read.

It is with heartfelt thanks that we have put in these "brief history stories" to give a glimpse of some of the group's own Blaxhall memories. These have been written by each individual.

And I am sorry that Bert Smith with his cheeky smile is not here to see this book come off the press.

# RAYMOND POACHER

## Born Blaxhall, 1928

I was born in Blaxhall at No.2 High Terrace and moved to No. 1 when I was two years old, where I lived until I was 18.

I started at Blaxhall School at five years walked with brothers George and Albert in all weathers. School summer holidays sometimes mother would give us a bottle of water and sandwiches and send us down to Langham river for the day to get us out of the house.

Other things we would do was chasing rabbits on the harvest field with sticks. When blackberry picking time we would pick as many as possible and sell these to Mr Taylor at the Stone Common shop. At ten years old I started work for Mr Taylor at 2/6 a week delivering goods on a tradesman's bike with a basket on the front.

When I was 11 I started school at Wickham Market and left the shop job, and brother Albert took the job.

I then started work at the Rectory one hour before school and one hour after school and all day Saturday for 7/6 pence, which mother took and gave me sixpence, she needed the money for school clothes.

I left school at 14 and started work at Stone Farm, looking after the young stock in the mornings and on the fields for four hours and back to feeding before five o'clock. I done this for two years, I then went to work at Snape Maltings for two years, at 18 went and joined the army, in the Royal Artillery for three years.

I met Kathy my wife in 1947 and married 1948. Lived in Ilford in Essex, then retired back to Blaxhall when I was 65.

Raymond after his first Army haircut, c. 1946.

Raymond relaxing outside Tudor Cottage, Blaxhall c. 1950s.

# BERT SMITH

## Born Blaxhall, 1922

August Holidays when we were kids were happy days, the sun always seemed to shine and when we were able to slip away from chores we virtually ran wild.

Off to the harvest fields chasing rabbits, or in the woods climbing trees and making bows and arrows, but it all ended when we had to go blackberrying.

We would go out and fill buckets with blackberries and fill the zinc bath then sell them to Mr Tyler at Tunstall to help with paying for new shoes for school.

Bert aged about ten years old.

Bert Smith with Stella his daughter in his arms and young George Poacher outside Tudor Cottage, c.1950s.

A day out at Felixstowe, c. 1950s.

# DAPHNE GANT

## (née Savage)

### Born Iken, 1938

This photograph was taken outside of Acorn Cottage, Blaxhall in 1943. I'm standing beside my mother, Violet Savage (née Bennett) and brother Arnold. When my father Lenny went to war we were all living at Decoy House, Iken with my Nana and Grandad Bennett, where I was born.

Iken was evacuated for a battle area for the war, everyone had to get out quick. Nana and Grandad put all their furniture in a big shed at Dunningworth Hall Farm and went to live at Pump Square, Blaxhall with Auntie Poppy and children. Her husband Russell Savage was in the war.

We lived in part of Acorn Cottage with Uncle George Bennett next door to Mr and Mrs Derek Edwards and family. It was divided by locked doors. Mr Mattinson took this photograph for my mother to send to father to cheer him up.

After the war we moved to Snape.

Young Daphne and brother Arthur with their mother outside Acorn Cottage, c. 1944.

Daphne with John and Barney the horse.

# VIOLET SKEET
(née Edwards)

## Born Blaxhall, 1940

I was born at Acorn Cottage at the beginning of the Second World War. During the war, there would be soldiers sitting alongside Langham Road under the oak trees, cheerful land girls who worked on the farm and the prisoners of war who made elephants from grey blanket material, in exchange for bread baked by my mother. I remember the German who crashed his plane and landed in a tree at the back of our house and provided us with lovely parachute material.

We always had fresh vegetables from our large garden and meat from the rabbits - some shot with my Father's "Long Margaret" 12 bore shot gun.

We did not have pocket money, but could earn money picking blackberries, collecting acorns and singling out sugar beet. We had to go to the Rectory for chocolate powder and malt.

I had a pet ferret that would follow me everywhere. I remember passing notes under the landing door to our neighbours children - Daphne and Arnold. We made bows with string across and arrows from the thatched roof. We fished and swam at Langham River - I fell in once before I had learnt to swim and was pulled out by Charlie Ling.

I was upset on leaving Blaxhall School finding I had to cycle to Saxmundham and take the bus to Leiston Grammar School when most of my friends went to Wickham Market School.

There was much sadness when my brother Roy was killed in a road accident aged 19, shortly after being confirmed with my brother Peter and myself at Snape Church.

We had no electricity until 1955-56 but we were always warm, clean and well fed. We had strict discipline instilling respect for others . Christmas was always a happy time but not Guy Fawkes as we were living in a house with a thatched roof!

I love the countryside and am now retired back to the area where I was born.

Violet aged three years.

Violet receives her bursary from the Ipswich Health District, 1979.

# PETER FLETCHER

## Born Blaxhall, 1914

When I left school at Easter 1929 the Depression of the early '30s was in the offing and jobs were few and far between. However in July I got a job at Garretts of Leiston but in January of 1931 the works went broke and we were all on the dole. We were now in the grip of the Depression and most of the men in Blaxhall were unemployed. We used to walk to Saxmundham twice a week to sign on the dole. Things gradually improved and in January 1932 Garretts was purchased by Beyer and Peacock of Manchester and I returned to work.

After the war Garretts obtained a contract to build peat harvesting equipment for the Southern Irish government. At the beginning of June 1956 I was sent to southern Ireland to repair these machines which were showing signs of wear and tear. As about 120 machines were involved, this was quite a long job and we were out there until the middle of September. Luckily it was a hot dry summer as most of the work was out of doors.

I was the first person in Blaxhall to own a motorbike, this was in July 1929. It was a 1925 350cc

Peter (right) on peat trenching machine, southern Ireland, June 1956.

Triumph and it cost £17 which was quite a bit of money in those days, I was only 15 years old at the time.

In 1931 I exchanged it for a new 250cc O.H.V Triumph at a cost of £29. While the old machine was only fitted with acetylene lighting the new one had electric lighting, which was much brighter. I had this machine for four years until 1935 when I obtained a new Vincent H.R.D 500cc O.H.V machine at a cost of £80. This was the first make of machine in Britain to be built with a sprung rear frame making for a much more comfortable ride. After two years in 1937 I exchanged two wheels for four and after eight years that was the end of my motor-cycling days.

Peter on his new 250cc Triumph, 1931.

# MARY SMITH
## (née Price)

### Born Blaxhall, 1922

I was born at Stone Common in the house what is now called Greenbanks.

I was nine when we moved to Cherry Tree Cottage.

The shop was great at Christmas I loved to see what was in the window.

I liked living on Stone Common.

RIGHT: Mary at seventeen.
BELOW: On Stone Common feeding the geese, c. 1932.

# PERCY DREWERY

## Born Blaxhall, 1926

Looking at the photograph of us on the harvest field, waiting for the rabbits to run, reminds me of the happy and carefree days we all enjoyed.

Money was short but we never went to bed hungry; not in our household anyway. There were seven of us; Mum and Dad and five children. I remember Dad having to cycle to Trimley every day to pull sugar beet, just to provide food for us all. I also remember the day I found him dead at the bottom of the stairs, December 24th 1939, I was just 13 years old - not a very good Christmas that year.

The evacuees arrived in the village and we soon all became friends. The four names I remember most were Joan and Reggie Lygo, Gerald Rickards and Victor Robertson. I wonder where they are now?

I left school at the age of 14 to work on the Cobbold Estate at Blaxhall Hall Farm. I left there at the age of 17 to work in Ipswich but I didn't like town life so came home after seven weeks to work on the land again at Red House Farm, Blaxhall. I again left there at the age of 17 to work on the forestry. I was then called up at the age of 18 and after training I joined the Parachute Regiment where I saw service in Germany and Palestine.

Percy in uniform, 1945.

I could go on about my life; getting married having a family and so on but it would take too long, so there I must end.

Percy (front right) rabbiting during harvest.

# HENRY HAMMOND

## Born Blaxhall, 1934

I started at Blaxhall School at 4½ years old with my sister Ena, I can remember we used to cut across Mr Sherwood's field and come out at the White House, that used to save about ten minutes walking time.

When harvest holidays came around I used to go with my father up to Stone Farm and drive the horse and waggon from the stack to the field to be loaded with sheaves.

On Sunday there used to be Sunday School at the church but I did not like that so I would hide up and pretend that I didn't know the time. I left school at 15 years and started work at Lord Graham's Chantry Farm, Campsey Ash, cleaning Lord Graham's shoes, getting sticks and wood in for the fire, then make the day up in the garden and looking after the chickens.

At 18 years I was called up for National Service and spent some time in Germany and South

Henry in uniform, 1952.

Korea. I was in the 1st Battalion Essex Regiment and finished my service in Korea. I met my wife Glenda in 1953 at Darsham Fox the local pub and we got married in 1956 and we had three sons.

Henry and Glenda Hammond's wedding, 1956.

# ENA PLANT
## (née Hammond)

### Born Blaxhall, 1932

I was born at the Old Barn, Blaxhall. I went to Blaxhall school, which is now a Youth Hostel on the hill. After leaving Blaxhall School I then went to Tunstall for a while.

While at school I used to go blackberry picking with my grandmother, then off to clean her house and do the washing up which had been left for a week, as she worked at the canning factory in Tunstall. I would earn 2/6 a week. After I left Tunstall school I worked at Glemham Hall for Lady Blanche Cobbold in the big house which has as many windows in as the days of the year.

RIGHT: Ena (left) with grandmother Trui Reeve, Ena's mother Lily and son Michael.

Ena with her father and son Michael.

# SHANE PICTOR

## Born Ipswich, 1972

Being two generations younger than many of my BAG fellows I obviously have some very different memories, but nevertheless have still witnessed much change and one or two interesting events.

Perhaps most telling is the apparent passing of an era, as I can recall several things that changed irreversibly in my lifetime. The first is the village shop; there were no less than three when I was five years old, but that was reduced to one within a couple of years. The last one though still received regular visits from myself and a friend, mounted on bicycles, to purchase penny sweets, bottles of drink, or oddments of shopping needed by our parents. That too is now long since gone.

Another image common in my childhood but now virtually gone is that of old men in flat caps and Norfolk jackets; they could still be found all over Blaxhall in the early 1980s, digging allotments, feeding fowl, chatting on corners, but now you're lucky to see one or two during a day in the village.

Shane (centre) and friend Luke ready for a sponsored cycle ride. Clara Jenkins and Grandad Fred Mayhew look on.

The most exciting memory I have has to be the demise of Church Farm farmhouse; being only a child I was both scared and fascinated when my grandfather told me there was a house on fire up the road. Almost as exciting was the storm of 1987, but somehow weather was taken more in our stride back then; I vividly remember my disappointment at the sight of the school bus lumbering through the passage between 4ft snowdrifts, realising a day off school wasn't on the cards after all. Proof, after all, that some things never change.

BELOW: Shane describes the intricacies of 'The Blaxhall Family Tree' at one of the BAG events.

Peter Fletcher and Ena Plant at a BAG meeting November 2006.

Henry Hammond and Ray Poacher discussing the identity of individuals seen in a local photograph.

A local family help identify some of the individuals in the Group's photograph database.

During the time of the Local Heritage Initiative project, which culminated in the production of this book, the Blaxhall Archive Group held several events in the village hall. In January 2006 Bridget Hanley (centre), archivist at the Suffolk Records Office, gave a talk about the Rope family archives held at the SRO.

# CHAPTER ONE
# PEOPLE AND PLACES

## Part 1 - Where people lived

How far back shall we start our story? Although there is evidence of both Neolithic and Bronze age man and then later Roman influence throughout the area we now know as Blaxhall, perhaps the early Anglo-Saxon period is a good place to begin.

This was the period once known as the 'Dark Ages' when the Roman legions had returned to mainland Europe in 409AD and new peoples such as the Angles, Saxons and Jutes were beginning to move into the void left by Rome.

Waterborne transport was the most important way of getting about at that time and, and what with a higher sea level and no river walls, the nearby River Alde would have been very much wider and somewhat deeper than today. Because of the river's importance a good habitation site needed easy access to the water and, although over the last 1500 years the river has receded to its present day

channel, those early sites can still be pinpointed as they hug the 10 to 15 metre contour line along the river's southern shore. Today, these early sites are probably marked by the farmsteads of Red House Farm, Blaxhall Hall Farm, Glebe Farm, Fir Tree Farm and Grove Farm as you can see below in Figure 1.

There is also evidence of an early 6th century cemetery, which might in fact mark the site of the first Blaxhall. The name 'Blaxhall' is thought to derive from 'Blaca' (an Anglo-Saxon settler) and 'halh' (Old English: 'nook or corner') - 'Blaca's halh'. If you look again at the map in Figure 1, particularly the south-west corner, you will see how the contours mark out an inlet, nook or corner, sheltered from the winds and not immediately obvious to ship-borne invaders. Perhaps the cemetery was sited here intentionally; visible from both river and tracks it would reinforce the fact that this was Blaca's patch!

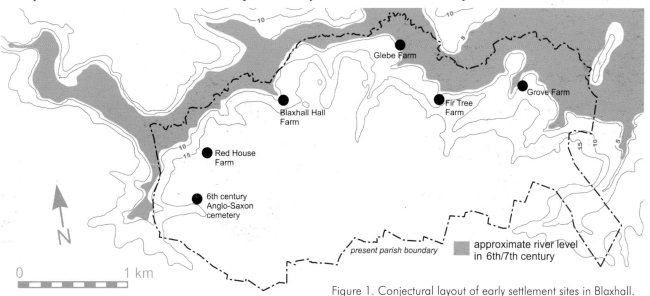

Figure 1. Conjectural layout of early settlement sites in Blaxhall.

Other local place names give clues to a wilder, wetter landscape: Beversham – 'the place where the beavers live' and Bordun Hill – 'boar's hill' (a name now lost and which describes the high ground above Fir Tree Farm).

We move on five centuries and find the name of Blaxhall recorded in the Domesday Book of 1086. There were five tenants-in-chief holding amongst them 263 acres; and these 263 acres were divided into 19 separate tenancies. Earl Alan owned four of these tenancies which were held by Hamo de Valenis; a name which is remembered in the medieval Blaxhall manor of Valence, which had land in Blaxhall, Tunstall and Wantisden.

Roger Bigod (1st Earl of Norfolk) had four small estates totalling 66 acres worked by eight freemen with names such as Ulf and Alwin. From these small estates the manor of Blaxhall Hall was formed.

One early lord of Blaxhall Hall was Thomas de Weyland, who seems to have been a bit of a rogue. A Plea of 1290 records a *"complaint from Robert de Saxmundeham, parson; that Richard de Weyland, Thomas de Weyland and others, broke the doors and, forcibly entered his dwelling place and carried away his goods"*. For this misdemeanour Thomas abjured the realm for felony and the manor was taken into the King's hands. The de Weylands did eventually get their lands back and held them until 1370.

## Medieval Blaxhall

During the medieval period records for Blaxhall are relatively scarce and most information comes from government tax returns and other legal documents. Some of the surnames are mentioned frequently in these documents but have since disappeared, whereas a few we still recognise in the village today. During the 1300s surnames such as Deth (one Deth, a servant of the Earl of Ufford was assaulted here in 1327), other surnames such as Myles and Osbern were numerous, and there was one Cutting.

In the 1400s surnames such as Osbern and Knight crop up often, with one reference to a Heryng. By the 1500s Myles and Osbern are still mentioned often, as well as the surnames Shepperd and Fleet, the latter being remembered in a Stone Farm field named – 'The Fleets'.

## Blaxhall around 1650

By the turn of the 17th century Blaxhall was a countryside in transition – what was left of the common field strip farming was being converted into a patchwork of small hedged fields called 'closes' or 'wents'. A small part of Blaxhall has been recorded on a map of 1601, Figure 2, and it shows some common fields remaining amongst the small hedged closes. At this time local farmers like John Corbould (who lived in Old Farm, Blaxhall) and

The site of Acorn Cottage probably dates back to the 17th century. This photograph was taken around the turn of the 19/20th cent.

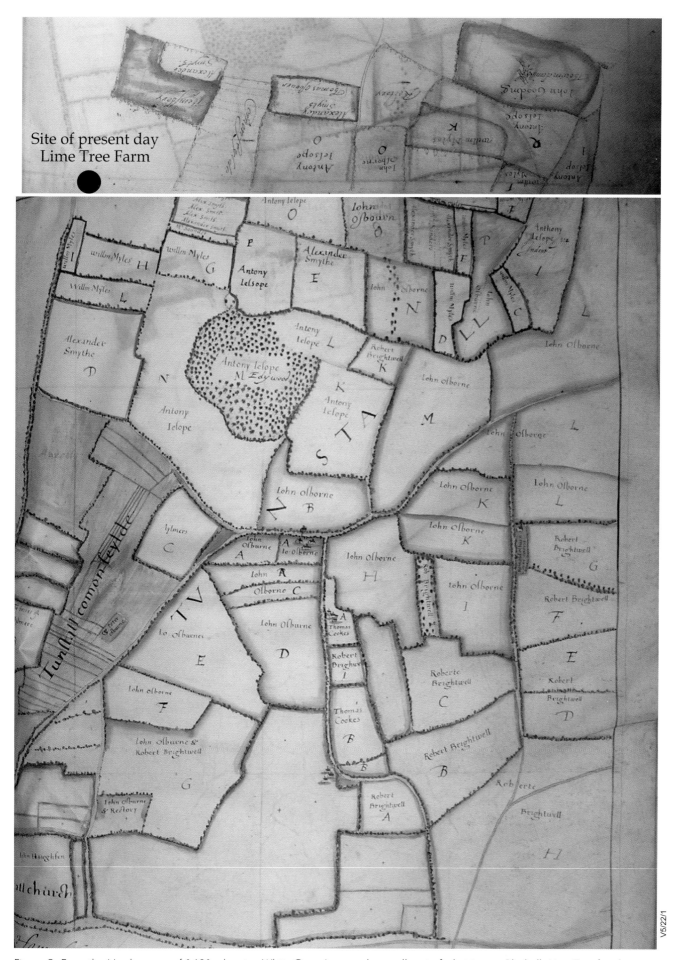

Site of present day
Lime Tree Farm

V5/22/1

Figure 2. From the Norden map of 1601, showing White Cross Lane and a small part of what is now Blaxhall. Lime Tree farmhouse would be approximately where William Myles (H) and (I) are marked in the top lefthand corner.

The site of these cottages in Langham Road probably dates back to the 17th century.

Edward Gould (who lived at Fir Tree Farm), were buying, selling and swapping individual common field strips to consolidate their holdings and in the process created the farms we recognise today.

Although reliable population figures are not available for such an early date as the 17th century, it is possible to make a cautious guess as to how many people lived in Blaxhall. For example, using the 1674 Hearth Tax Returns[1] and also some contemporary literature, we can be fairly certain that by the mid to late 17th century there were between 27 and 31 households. There is no agreed figure for an average number of people in a household in 17th century Suffolk; it could be as low as three or as high as six. Nationally, the population in the mid 17th century was stable or in slight decline, so if Blaxhall reflected the national trend, then perhaps a figure of four persons per household would not be far out. This would equate to Blaxhall having a population of around 125 by 1650.

The distribution of these 30-odd households throughout the parish is also difficult to know but fieldwork and research into contemporary documents has produced a layout as shown in Figure 3. All the farm sites that exist today existed then plus a few small farmsteads that have since disappeared. Two windmills, a workhouse and a brick kiln have all faded from the landscape (although the workhouse remains as a private residence). Of the individual cottages some still exist whilst others have vanished and only a darkened patch in the field and some pieces of pottery mark their original sites.

## Boom time

From about 1750 the population of England had started to increase exponentially, which meant by 1851 it had practically tripled. Blaxhall reflected this national trend; the parish total of 180 in 1750 had become 577 souls by 1851 – a threefold increase. Where did all these new people live? The simple answer is that there was substantial encroachment onto two of the Blaxhall commons – Mill Common and Stone Common (see endpapers). In Figure 4, an 1809 map drawn by T. Cole[2] for Sir Dudley North of Glemham Hall, shows the two commons;

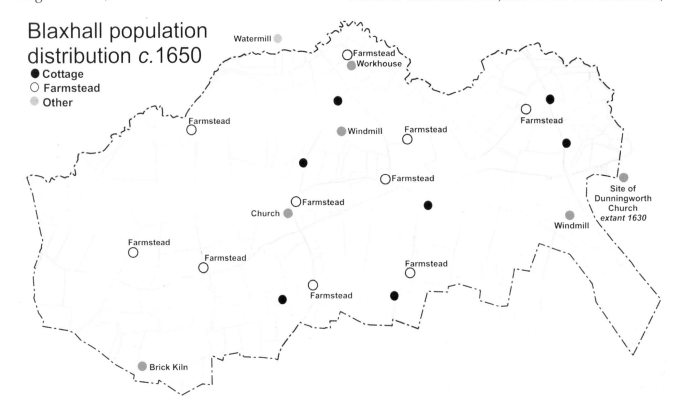

Figure 3. Conjectural distribution of farmsteads and cottages in the mid-17th century.

[1] see References page 154

three or four cottages, plus a windmill on Mill Common and six households on Stone Common, known then as Church Common. The same two are shown again as they were in 1836 and they show, quite graphically, how major encroachment onto the two commons had absorbed the extra people in just 30 years.

This huge rise in population put considerable strain on the rural society. Some areas of the country were able to absorb this increase but food production particularly in the south and east of England found it hard to keep pace and profound poverty was the immediate outcome.

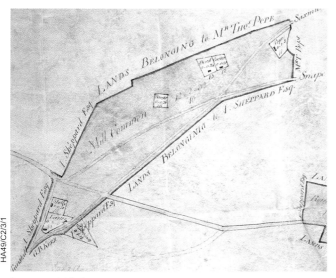

Figure 4. Mill Common in 1809.

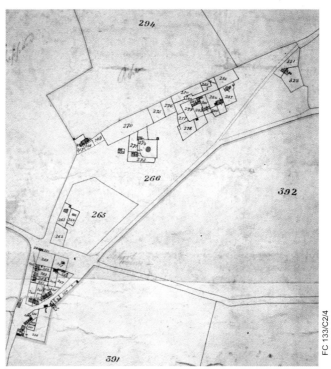

Mill Common in 1836. Additional houses have grown around the two earlier focal points.

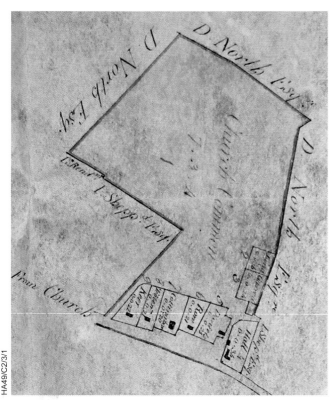

Stone Common (then known as Church Common) in 1809.

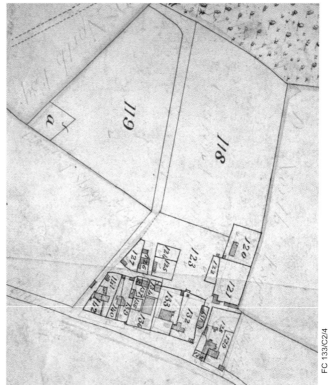

Stone Common, less than 30 years later in 1836. Note the major encroachment around the original settlements.

## Hard times

The 1831 national Census Return gives a total of 525 people in Blaxhall, a rise of over 70% since 1801. What work or subsistence these people found to support themselves is difficult to imagine. A list of the poor of Blaxhall, Figure 5, was drawn up by Sir Dudley North in 1829. It gives the name of the head of the household, family size and what they were to receive from a £50 legacy. Table 1 is a transcribed copy of that list which totals 302 individuals living in the parish, a figure that represents something like 58% of the inhabitants deemed, by 19th century standards, to be so poor as to be in need of financial support.

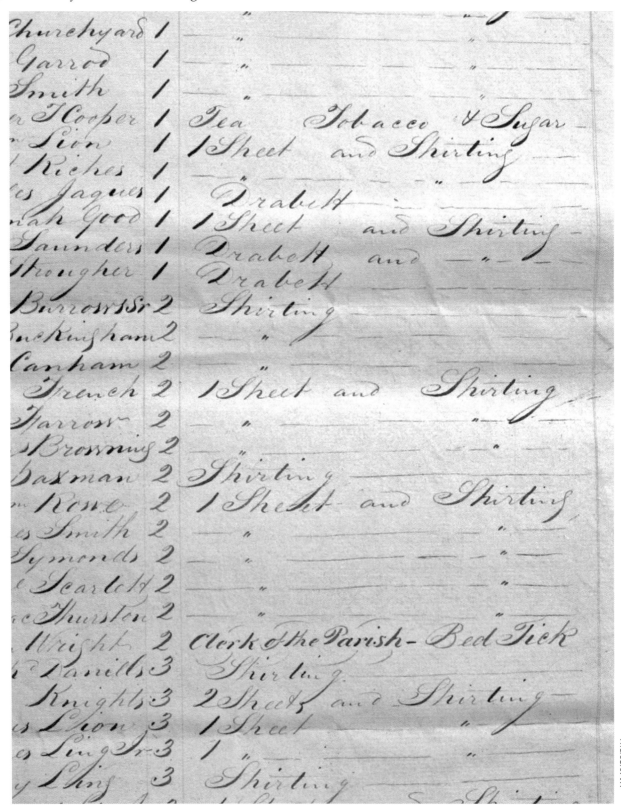

Figure 5. Front page from 'List of the Poor of Blaxhall', 1829.

Table 1. Transcribed version of 'A List of the Poor Blaxhall, 1829'.

| Number in Family | | | £ | s | d |
|---|---|---|---|---|---|
| Widow Brown | 1 | 1 Sheet & Shirting | 0 | 5 | 0 |
| Widow Blanden | 1 | 1 Sheet & Shirting | 0 | 5 | 0 |
| Widow Garrod | 1 | 1 Sheet & Shirting | 0 | 5 | 0 |
| Widow Smith | 1 | 1 Sheet & Shirting | 0 | 5 | 0 |
| Widower J Cooper | 1 | 1 Tea Tobacco & sugar | 0 | 5 | 0 |
| Willm Sion | 1 | 1 Sheet & Shirting | 0 | 5 | 0 |
| Rob Riches | 1 | 1 Sheet & Shirting | 0 | 5 | 0 |
| Miles Jaques | 1 | 1 Drabett | 0 | 5 | 0 |
| Hannah Good | 1 | 1 Sheet & Shirting | 0 | 5 | 0 |
| Boy Saunders | 1 | 1 Drabett & Shirting | 0 | 5 | 0 |
| Boy Strougher | 1 | 1 Drabett | 0 | 5 | 0 |
| John Burrows Sr | 2 | 1 Shirting | 0 | 6 | 0 |
| John Buckingham | 2 | 1 Shirting | 0 | 6 | 0 |
| Thos Canham | 2 | 1 Shirting | 0 | 6 | 0 |
| John French | 2 | 1 Sheet & Shirting | 0 | 6 | 0 |
| Joe Farrow | 2 | 1 Sheet & Shirting | 0 | 6 | 0 |
| Frans Browning | 2 | 1 Sheet & Shirting | 0 | 6 | 0 |
| Adm Paxman | 2 | 1 Shirting | 0 | 6 | 0 |
| Willm Rowe | 2 | 1 Sheet & Shirting | 0 | 6 | 0 |
| James Smith | 2 | 1 Sheet & Shirting | 0 | 6 | 0 |
| James Symonds | 2 | 1 Sheet & Shirting | 0 | 6 | 0 |
| ? | 2 | 1 Sheet & Shirting | 0 | 6 | 0 |
| Isaac Thurston | 2 | 1 Sheet & Shirting | 0 | 6 | 0 |
| John Knight | 2 | Bed Tick | 0 | 12 | 0 |
| Richard Daniels | 3 | 1Shirting | 0 | 8 | 0 |
| John Knights | 3 | 2 Sheets & Shirting | 0 | 8 | 0 |
| James Lion | 3 | 1 Sheet & Shirting | 0 | 8 | 0 |
| James Ling jnr | 3 | 1 Sheet & Shirting | 0 | 8 | 0 |
| Mary Ling | 3 | 1 Shirting | 0 | 8 | 0 |
| Samuel Ling jnr | 3 | 1 Sheet & Shirting | 0 | 8 | 0 |
| Widow Ling | 3 | 1 Sheet & Shirting | 0 | 8 | 0 |
| Robert ? | 3 | 1 Sheet & Shirting | 0 | 8 | 0 |
| Robert ? | 3 | 1 Sheet & Shirting | 0 | 8 | 0 |
| Henry Newson | 3 | 2 Sheets & Shirting | 0 | 8 | 0 |
| Samuel Wyart | 3 | 2 Sheets & Shirting | 0 | 8 | 0 |
| James Knights | 3 | 1 Shirting | 0 | 8 | 0 |
| John Cable | 3 | 2 Sheets & Shirting | 0 | 13 | 0 |
| Samuel Bird | 4 | 2 Sheets & Shiritng | 0 | 10 | 6 |
| John Burrows Jnr | 4 | 2 Sheets & Shirting | 0 | 10 | 6 |
| Keer Browning | 4 | 2 Sheets & Shirting | 0 | 10 | 6 |
| Abraham Curtis | 4 | 2 Sheets & Shirting | 0 | 10 | 6 |
| John Cable Jnr | 4 | 2 Sheets & Shirting | 0 | 10 | 6 |
| William Forsdyke | 4 | 2 Sheets & Shirting | 0 | 10 | 6 |
| Joe Farrow jnr | 4 | 2 Sheets & Shirting | 0 | 10 | 6 |
| John Paxman | 4 | 1 Drabett | 0 | 10 | 6 |
| Thomas Smy | 4 | 1 Sheet & Shirting | | | |
| Henry Baskett | 5 | 3 Sheets & Shirting | 0 | 13 | 0 |
| John Cable | 5 | 2 Sheets & Shirting | 0 | 13 | 0 |
| Robert Knights | 5 | 2 Sheets & Shirting | 0 | 13 | 0 |
| Joseph ? | 5 | 2 Sheets & Shirting | 0 | 13 | 0 |
| Susan Poacher | 5 | 2 Sheets & Drabett | 0 | 13 | 0 |

| Number in Family | | | £ | s | d |
|---|---|---|---|---|---|
| Richard Puttock | 5 | 2 Sheets & Shirting | 0 | 13 | 0 |
| Lionel Riches | 5 | 2 Sheets & Flannell & Do. | 0 | 13 | 0 |
| Gorrin Scarces | 5 | 2 Drabett & Shirting | 0 | 13 | 0 |
| David Ling Snr | 5 | 1 Drabett & Shirting | 0 | 13 | 0 |
| William Burrows | 6 | 1 Bed Tick & Shirting | 0 | 15 | 0 |
| William Bailey | 6 | 2 Sheets & Shirting | 0 | 15 | 0 |
| John Cole | 6 | 2 Sheets & Shirting | 0 | 15 | 0 |
| John Hammond | 6 | 2 Sheets & Shirtng | 0 | 15 | 0 |
| John Keer | 6 | 2 Drabett & Shirting | 0 | 15 | 0 |
| William Newson | 6 | 2 Sheets & Shirting | 0 | 15 | 0 |
| James Newson | 6 | 2 Sheets & Shirting | 0 | 15 | 0 |
| Thomas Plant snr | 6 | 2 Sheets & Shirting | 0 | 15 | 0 |
| Thomas Plant jnr | 6 | 2 Sheets & Drabett | 0 | 15 | 0 |
| Isaac Moor | 7 | 3 Sheets & Shirting | 0 | 18 | 0 |
| ? Newson | 7 | 3 Sheets & Shirting | 0 | 18 | 0 |
| Spar K Smith | 7 | 4 Sheets & Shirting | 0 | 18 | 0 |
| John Wardley | 7 | 2 Sheets, Drabett & Shirting | 0 | 18 | 0 |
| John ? | 8 | 2 Sheets, Drabett & Shirting | 1 | 0 | 0 |
| William Ling | 8 | 4 Sheets & Shirting | 1 | 0 | 0 |
| John ? Ling | 8 | 4 Sheets & Shirting | 1 | 0 | 0 |
| James Thurston | 8 | 2 Sheets Drabett & Shirting | 1 | 0 | 0 |
| James Ling Snr | 9 | 4 Sheets Drabett & Shirting | 1 | 4 | 0 |
| George Ling | 10 | 4 Sheets Drabett & Shirting | 1 | 7 | 0 |
| James Ling Snr | 11 | 4 Sheets Drabett & Shirting | 1 | 10 | 0 |

| | | | £ | s | d |
|---|---|---|---|---|---|
| Sub-Total | **302 Persons** | | | | |

**Not Resident in Parish**

| Number in Family | | | £ | s | d |
|---|---|---|---|---|---|
| Girl Page | 1 | 1 Flannell & Shirting | 0 | 5 | 0 |
| Widow Harris | 1 | 1 Sheet & Shirting | 0 | 5 | 0 |
| Widow ? | 1 | 1 Flannell & Shirting | 0 | 5 | 0 |
| Widow Rowe | 2 | 1 Flannell & Shirting | 0 | 6 | 0 |
| John Burrell | 2 | 1 Drabett & Shirting | 0 | 6 | 0 |
| Thomas Aldrich | 2 | 1 Sheet & Shirting | 0 | 6 | 0 |
| John Smy | 2 | 1 Drabett & Shirting | 0 | 6 | 0 |
| William Tyler | 2 | 1 Flannell & Shirting | 0 | 6 | 0 |
| John Ling | 5 | 2 Sheets & Shirting | 0 | 13 | 0 |
| William Scarse | 5 | 2 Sheets Blankett Shirting | 0 | 13 | 0 |
| Thomas Harris | 6 | 2 Sheets Blankett Shirting | 0 | 13 | 0 |
| Thomas Hearn | 6 | 2 Sheets Blankett Shirting | 0 | 13 | 0 |
| William Leach | 6 | 2 Sheets Blankett Shirting | 0 | 13 | 0 |
| James Pallant | 9 | 2 Sheets 2 Blanketts shirting & Twill | 0 | 14 | 0 |

| | | | £ | s | d |
|---|---|---|---|---|---|
| Sub - Total | **352Persons** | | 48 | 10 | 6 |
| David Ling jnr | 3 | Blankett & Shirting | 0 | 8 | 0 |
| ? | 6 | 2 Sheets & Shirting | 0 | 8 | 6 |
| ? | 5 | 2 Sheets & Shirting | 0 | 13 | 0 |
| **TOTAL 366 Persons** | | | 50 | 0 | 0 |

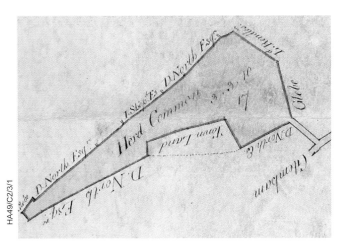

HA49/C2/3/1

In 1809 the area was known as Herd Common or sometimes Water Common. The workhouse had probably been there since the 1600s and once it had closed in the 1830s the area became known as Workhouse Common!

## The Blaxhall workhouse and the old Poor Law

The offices of churchwarden and overseer of the poor were defined in the Great Poor Law of 1601. Both offices were elected on a yearly basis from the more substantial householders of the parish.

Each parish was a self governing body responsible for its own poor people. All the money required for the upkeep of the parish poor was raised by the parishioners and it was the parish officer's duty to collect this money by means of the poor rate. The overseer of the poor was expected when necessary to feed, clothe, house and find work for his poor inhabitants. He apprenticed the pauper children and, with the aid of the parish constable, rigorously pursued the absconding fathers of illegitimate children.

The Blaxhall workhouse (now Gorse Farm), was situated on what was then known as Herd Common. The thatch and timber part of the original building (see photograph on page 20), probably dates from the 17th century. It is not known if it was built for the role of workhouse or if an existing building was requisitioned for the purpose. An account book for the years 1740 to 1760 still exists in the Suffolk Records Office, and an expenditure page is shown here in Figure 6. John Pope, a farmer from Grove Farm, was the overseer at this date. Note the reference to 'flags' – which in those days was not a reference to paving, flowers or bunting but referred to long strips of heather root which were used as a source of fuel before coal became widely available. Molly Pictor of Stone Common remembers her father, over fifty years ago, referring to the strips of grass cut and

IRO/K681/1/44/7

The old workhouse became known as Workhouse Cottages seen here c.1920s. Now known as Gorse Farm.

Figure 6. A page from the 'Overseer's Account Book' for 1749.

FC 133/G1/1

laid aside when digging were known as 'flags'; so the term lived on for some appreciable time after coal had become the only source of fuel and heather burning for warmth was just a memory.

The workhouse was in existence until 1834 when the Poor Law Unions were created as part of the new Victorian Poor Law passed in that year. Responsibility for the poor passed to the Board of Guardians of the various unions. The Plomesgate

Union workhouse was built in Wickham Market in 1836/7 and the poor of Blaxhall were sent there after that date.

## Settlement and Removal Orders

The overseer of the poor's most important duty was to protect his parish from the claims of paupers who were not his responsibility. To aid the enforcement of the Act and also the overseer in the pursuance of his duty, the first Settlement Law of 1662 was passed which allowed any stranger to be removed from a parish if he or she did not pay £10 or more in rent, or did not find a means of security to indemnify the parish against any expense incurred by the said stranger. Temporary visitors were obliged to provide a certificate from their parish stating that they would be received back again if the individual fell on hard times.

A number of these 'Settlement Orders'[3] concerning Blaxhall still exist and are held in the Suffolk Records Office. The relevant details are shown in Table 2 and Table 3, and although it is only a list of names, each settlement order must represent all sorts of human emotions from trials and tribulations; hope and joy to sadness and trepidation.

Table 2. Settlement Orders of individuals moving to or from Blaxhall

## Settlement Orders

| Year | Name | Occupation | Wife | Children | Parish of legal settlement | Destination settlement parish |
|------|------|-----------|------|----------|---------------------------|-------------------------------|
| 1753 | John Daniel | | Sarah | | St.Margaret's, Ipswich | Blaxhall |
| 1762 | Thomas Newson | Carpenter | Sarah | | Blaxhall | Little Glemham |
| 1765 | William Cady | | Sarah | Sarah | Blaxhall | Iken |
| 1767 | John Cracknall | Labourer | Mary | | Blaxhall | Iken |
| 1767 | John Kemp | Shoemaker | Elizabeth | | Blaxhall | Snape |
| 1776 | John Wright | | Martha | | Little Glemham | Blaxhall |
| 1778 | John Blandell | | Margaret | | Blaxhall | Snape |
| 1780 | Sarah Bealey | | | William | Little Glemham | Blaxhall |
| 1791 | Robert Jacobs | | Ann | | Orford | Blaxhall |
| 1791 | Robert Symonds | Labourer | Mary | James | Little Glemham | Blaxhall |
| 1791 | Henry Scarlett | | Martha | Martha | Little Glemham | Blaxhall |
| 1791 | William Clouting | | Lucy | | Little Glemham | Blaxhall |
| 1826 | James Thurston | | Lydia | James, Harriet, Lydia, Sophia, John, William, Isaac & Robert | Sibton | Blaxhall |

Table 3. Removal Orders of individuals moving to or from Blaxhall.

# Removal Orders

| Year | Name | Occupation | Wife | Children | Removed to | Removed from |
|---|---|---|---|---|---|---|
| 1735 | Thomas Archer | Husbandman | Ann | | Blaxhall | Little Glemham |
| 1801 | Mary Weavers | Singlewoman | | | Blaxhall | Chillesford |
| 1801 | Thomas Rackham | Thatcher | Lettice | John, Thomas and an enfant | Blaxhall | Snape |
| 1803 | Elizabeth Thurston | Singlewoman | | | Blaxhall | Tunstall |
| 1805 | Elizabeth Farrow | Singlewoman | | | Marlesford | Blaxhall |
| 1806 | Cornelius Welton | | Elizabeth | Clarissa, Mary, William & George | Benhall | Blaxhall |
| 1807 | Sarah Johnson | Singlewoman | | | Blaxhall | Leiston |
| 1807 | James Cole | | Sarah | Sarah | Iken | Blaxhall |
| 1808 | Hannah Thurston | Singlewoman | | | St. Clement's, Norwich | Blaxhall |
| 1810 | Sarah Goodram | Singlewoman | | | Needham, Norfolk | Blaxhall |
| 1811 | William Forsdyke | Bricklayer | Mary | Frederick & Stephen | Blaxhall | Tunstall |
| 1817 | John Smith | | Hannah | Hannah, John, William, James, Sidney and enfant | Blaxhall | Yoxford |
| 1817 | Jonathan Ling | Labourer | Hannah | Hannah, James and Elisa | Butley | Blaxhall |
| 1817 | John Cunningham | | Alice | | Blaxhall | Wickham Market |
| 1817 | Mary Ling | Widow | | Mary Ann & Bathsheba | Blaxhall | Tunstall |
| 1817 | Honor Brown | Wife of a soldier | | Hannah | Blaxhall | Framlingham |
| 1817 | Samuel Funnel | An enfant | | | Blaxhall | Bredfield |
| 1819 | James Knight | | Ann | three children | Blaxhall | St. Mildred, Canterbury |
| 1819 | Mary Ling | Widow | | three children | Blaxhall | Aldeburgh |
| 1821 | George Forsdick | Labourer | | | Campsea Ashe | Blaxhall |
| 1822 | Benjamin Gaity | Labourer | | | Blaxhall | Eyke |
| 1823 | Mary Keeble | Singlewoman | | | Hollesley | Blaxhall |
| 1826 | William Scarce | Labourer | Alice | Harriet, William, Alice, Jenima | Blaxhall | Snape |
| 1827 | Rose Mower | Singlewoman | | | Blaxhall | Walpole |
| 1830 | John Ling | Labourer | Charlotte | Robert and Ann | Blaxhall | Little Glemham |
| 1830 | Harriet Curtis | Singlewoman | | | Wickham Market | Blaxhall |
| 1833 | Ann Page | Singlewoman | | | Blaxhall | Wickham Market |
| 1834 | David Smy | Labourer | | | Sudbourne | Blaxhall |
| 1846 | Edward Faiers | Labourer | | | Bradwell on Sea | Blaxhall |

There are a few records of apprenticeships, where overseers in other parishes have found a new life for an individual in Blaxhall. These records also give us the names of certain tradesmen working in Blaxhall in the 18th century.

Table 4. Poor boys sent as apprentices.

# Apprenticeships

| From | Date | Name | To whom indentured (all Blaxhall) | Occupation |
|---|---|---|---|---|
| Framlingham | 1691 | Thomas Flatt | Robert Bennett | Blacksmith |
| Sweffling | 1752 | Thomas Taylor, a poor child | Lional Coats | Thatcher |
| Orford | 1791 | Thomas Moore, a poor child | Robert Jacobs | Bricklayer |
| Framlingham | 1791 | William Dawson | Rev. Richard Taylor | Parson |
| Kettleburgh | 1814 | Lionel Groom, a poor child | Jonathan Larter | Boot & shoemaker |
| Blaxhall | 1825 | John Cole | Robert Scorfield, Co. Durham | Shipowner |
| Blaxhall | 1825 | William Saunders | Robert Scorfield, Co. Durham | Shipowner |

# Into the 20th century

By 1901 the parish population had declined to 536 from its peak of forty years before. A few additional houses had been built in the intervening years but generally the settlement distribution was similar to that of 1836.

By 1951 the population was down to 342 and some of the properties had become empty; by the 1960s several were derelict and were pulled down (six at Pump Square, three known as Poplar Tree Cottages and several others). New properties with their modern conveniences were now the preferred living accommodation; a small council estate was built in the village and old properties were demolished and modern replacements put in their place. The number of young children in the village reached a new low and the school proved difficult to support and finally closed in 1962. Increasing mobility by villagers and a radical change in shopping habits put pressure on the two remaining shops until they both finally closed.

By 2006 the population was at its lowest since the 17th century and the demographics had changed dramatically with the 'week-end cottage' representing 20% of the households, a new phenomenon.

Lullie and Bessie Ling at 1 High Terrace

Looking across to the Forge, Church Farm (thatched) and the village hall. The pit in the foreground was used by the children as a playground and also by the school for nature lessons and as a stage and backdrop for Shakespeare's 'A Midsummer Night's Dream' in the 1950s.

## Occupations

Traditionally, everyone worked in agriculture or was in a supporting trade like blacksmith or carpenter; and this had been a constant for many hundreds of years and has only changed recently within living memory.

Data taken from the national censuses of 1841 and 1901 plus a 2006 headcount is shown in Table 5 below, and illustrates very well how the occupational profile has changed over 160 years. It shows that in 1841 over 67% of the residents of Blaxhall were directly employed in agriculture. By 1901 the figure had reduced to around 55% but with many ancillary trades still depending on agriculture. The major change probably came about in the last quarter of the 20th century as the figure for 2006 shows that a mere 6.7% of Blaxhall residents now work in agriculture.

This phenonemon is just a part of the changes we have seen in modern society during the past fifty years. For example, supporting trades such as blacksmith, shoemaker, miller and draper have all evolved into different entities now to be found in the towns and industrial estates and no longer in the villages. Starting in the last years of the 20th century a major revolution is underway throughout the countryside – probably as profound as the changes around 1650 which we saw earlier in our story. It affects how we use the land and how we use the cottages and houses that lie within the countryside; and it is a revolution that still has some way to go.

Table 5. Change in occupations of Blaxhall residents.

| 1841 | % | 1901 | % | 2006 | % |
|------|-----|------|-----|------|-----|
| agricultural labourer | 60.7 | agricultural labourer | 22.9 | retired | 43.1 |
| retired | 11.2 | horseman | 16.1 | farmer | 5.0 |
| farmer | 5.2 | farmer | 5.7 | company director | 5.0 |
| shoemaker | 3.4 | shepherd | 4.8 | local government | 5.0 |
| gamekeeper | 3.4 | retired | 4.8 | engineer | 5.0 |
| carpenter | 2.6 | stockman | 3.8 | builder | 5.0 |
| shopkeeper | 1.7 | bricklayer | 3.8 | IT specialist | 3.3 |
| blacksmith | 1.7 | maltster labourer | 3.8 | window cleaner | 3.3 |
| shepherd | 1.7 | blacksmith | 3.8 | gardener | 3.3 |
| tailor | 1.7 | railway staff | 2.9 | secretary | 3.3 |
| rector | 0.9 | gamekeeper | 1.9 | graphic designer | 1.7 |
| pedlar | 0.9 | shopkeeper | 1.9 | bank manager | 1.7 |
| lathe renderer | 0.9 | gardener | 1.9 | hostel manager | 1.7 |
| bricklayer | 0.9 | coachman | 1.9 | teaching profession | 1.7 |
| miller | 0.9 | local government | 1.9 | chef | 1.7 |
| publican | 0.9 | shoemaker | 1.9 | factory worker | 1.7 |
| cooper | 0.9 | rector | 1.0 | carpenter | 1.7 |
| thatcher | 0.9 | pig dealer | 1.0 | publican | 1.7 |
| | | dressmaker | 1.0 | chemist | 1.7 |
| | | publican | 1.0 | builder's labourer | 1.7 |
| | | schoolmaster | 1.0 | agricultural labourer | 1.7 |
| | | traction engine driver | 1.0 | | |
| | | market gardener | 1.0 | | |
| | | roadman | 1.0 | | |
| | | thatcher | 1.0 | | |
| | | farm bailiff | 1.0 | | |
| | | carrier | 1.0 | | |
| | | hawker | 1.0 | | |
| | | molecatcher | 1.0 | | |
| | | postmaster | 1.0 | | |
| | | wheelwright | 1.0 | | |
| | | carpenter | 1.0 | | |
| | | shopworker | 1.0 | | |

## Age profile

The national Census Returns provide not only the number of individuals in each household but also their ages. This makes fascinating reading when the 1841 and 1901 information is compared to similar information for 2006. In Table 6 the three sets of figures of the ages of everybody in the Blaxhall population are compared and it can be seen that what was a 'young' population in 1841, with over 84% of the population being under 45 years of age, has turned completely around with over 60% of the population being over 45 years old in 2006.

Ullswater Estate workers c.1925. left to right: Abie Ling, Lawrence Fletcher and Fred Keeble.

Table 6. Breakdown of age groups at three dates.

| up to 1 year | 1 – 12 years | 13 – 21 years | 22 – 45 years | 46 – 65 years | 65+ years | census date |
|---|---|---|---|---|---|---|
| 3.3% | 34.4% | 20.5% | 26.3% | 11% | 4.5% | **1841 (575)** |
| 2.0% | 27.6% | 18.3% | 27.0% | 18.95 | 6.3% | **1901 (536)** |
| 0.7% | 7.4% | 3.0% | 28.1% | 50.4% | 10.4% | **2006 (135)** |

Tom Price, gamekeeper on the Glemham Estate, c. 1925.

Sawyers at work behind the Forge near Church Farm, c.1900. Left Darcher Poacher and Walter Reeve.

Workmen and machinery situated in the gravel pit (now the motocross). Lenny Savage is seen centre picture, covered in dust. The local council extracted gravel from the pit for upwards of twenty years.

# CHAPTER ONE
# PEOPLE AND PLACES

## Part 2 - Places where people lived and worked

## The Colossus of Mill Common

For most of the 19th century until its destruction in 1883, a huge post mill with roundhouse stood on Mill Common dominating that end of the village and to be seen for miles around the upper Alde valley. Windmills were a common feature of the countryside at that time; by the 1830s Suffolk had in excess of 450 of various types, with two-thirds of them being post mills and the majority being located on the eastern side of the county. Every village 'worth its corn' boasted at least one; some like Benhall and Snape locally had two. Blaxhall – not to be outdone – also had two post mills, the one on Mill Common and the other, curiously, outside the parish close to, and no doubt supplementing, Beversham Mill – "*The mill stands about 50 yards away from the main road and about 100 yard on the north side of the old watermill. This windmill is " called Blaxhall Mill"* wrote George A. Kenney in his *'Notes on Suffolk Windmills'*[4]; he referred in these notes to "Blaxhall(1)" as the Mill Common one and "Blaxhall(2)" as the one in Little Glemham, Beversham.  For clarity's sake, any further reference to Blaxhall Mill will be to the Mill Common one.

Post mills, one of the earliest forms of windmills and the most common in Suffolk, derived their name from the massive oak post on which the body, or 'buck' as it was called in Suffolk, was supported; this in turn was supported by a trestle of four quarter bars usually raised on brick piers to increase overall height and to reduce rot. Early post mills were usually "open trestle", but from the late 18th century onwards were more often built with a 'roundhouse' of brick or brick and flint

incorporating the piers, Figure 1. Unfortunately, there is no known depiction of Blaxhall Mill; the only representation of it is in a vignette in the lovely 1912 East window in St Peter's Church by Margaret Agnes Rope and her cousin, Margaret Aldrich Rope. Ada Mannall in her  notes interpreting the window says that the windmill was included, in the centre panel just above the Blessed Virgin's right shoulder, "to remember Blaxhall Mill".

What then were the credentials that made it so noteworthy?

Firstly, was its height. Brian Flint in *'Suffolk Windmills'*[5] on which this piece  draws freely, remarks that *"Blaxhall Mill was said to be very large and tall….. and may have vied for the title of the tallest post mill in Suffolk"*. This would mean it was well in excess of 50 feet high – the two highest documented post mills were Honington and Thorndon, while the one at Friston *"which measures 51 feet to the roof ridge is the tallest post mill still standing in the country"*.

Secondly, were its number of millstones. *"Most post mills had two pairs of stones, large mills sometimes three pairs whilst the big mill at Blaxhall had no less than four pairs, two in the head, two in the tail"* – the only Suffolk windmill to be identified with such a number. The most common size of millstone was four feet but they varied from three to five feet; it is not known what sizes our ones were, although judging from sections dug up a few years ago in the garden of the former miller's cottage, at least some of them were of the largest size. The majority of stones were of French 'burr', there being no suitable local stone, and were built up from sections

# Conventional layout of a post mill.

Figure 1. Layout and terms of a conventional post mill. Blaxhall Mill would have been built in the same style.

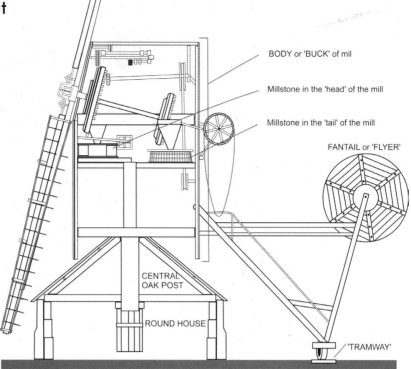

BODY or 'BUCK' of mil

Millstone in the 'head' of the mill

Millstone in the 'tail' of the mill

FANTAIL or 'FLYER'

CENTRAL OAK POST

ROUND HOUSE

'TRAMWAY'

of stone, cemented together and constrained with shrunk-on iron hoops.

Thirdly, there was its tramway. The fantail (see Figure 1), known as the 'flyer' in Suffolk, was for turning the mill to face the wind; it had six or eight blades mounted on a frame above the steps with the wheel carriage attached to the bottom of the steps, the tramwheel was of iron or sometimes wood. The tramway was of compacted earth, gravel or concrete…. *"whereas the large post mill at Blaxhall, burned in 1883, had an iron tramway which was then transferred to Brandeston mill which suffered a similar fate ten years later; it was finally taken to Pettaugh mill"*. The tramway (and wind tackle) were made by Collins of Melton at a cost of £70, c. £3500 in today's money! So, the tramway was a prized and valuable item, Blaxhall's being the only one mentioned in Mr. Flint's book.

From these credentials, it seems fair to conclude that Blaxhall Mill's reputation as *"very large and tall"* was well-founded. Indeed in George Ewart Evans's **'The Farm and the Village'**[6], this conclusion is confirmed by Jesse Lightman remarking that it was "the largest post mill in Suffolk". Jesse, born in 1907 in Brandeston, was apprenticed to the miller at Saxtead Green (which he restored for the Ministry of Works in the 1960s), and learnt his millwrighting at Whitmores, famous milling engineers in Wickham Market. He had, according to George Ewart Evans, a remarkable memory for anything connected with his craft and knew the history of most mills in East Anglia, even those that were flourishing during the 19th century, as he listened since he was a boy to the tales that the older millers had told him.

It has not yet been established exactly when our mill was built, the earliest known reference to date being found in the *Ipswich Journal* of 10th January 1807: *"to be sold by auction. All that windmill, lately erected and in full trade, now standing on Blaxhall Common and used by William Sawyer, the occupier thereof. Mr John Sawyer of Tunstall will show the premises"*. The words 'lately erected' are open to interpretation but seem to indicate that the mill had been built some time previously i.e. it was not newly built – it would not have been 'in full trade' if it were. 'The Shorter Oxford Dictionary based on Historical Principles' has one sense of 'lately' in this context as 'belonging to a recent period' and the meaning of 'recent' as 'belonging to a past period of time comparatively near to the present'; so it seems reasonable to suppose that the mill was built around the end of the 18th century.

We know from the above that our miller in 1807 was William Sawyer but it is not known for how long he had been 'the occupier thereof'. The auction that year resulted eventually in a sale to Samuel Browning who was known to be there by mid-1809, for he was the miller at the time of a tragic accident resulting in the death of the son of former miller William Sawyer[7]:

*"Eighteenth day of June 1809. Inquisition at the sign of the Ship in Blaxhall. Before John Wood, Gentleman, Coroner of the Liberty of Saint Etheldred on view of the body of Daniel Sawyer an Infant of the age of six years or*

Aerial view of the Mill site, early 1980's: the post mill was situated on the semi circular grass area now surrounded by a hedge which followed the outline of an artificial mound to raise the mill to better catch the wind. The mill's granary, right of picture, was converted to a private residence, with first floor added, shortly after the mill was burnt down; Peter Fletcher's grand-parents lived there from 1892. Mill Cottage is top of picture; Orchard (now Garden) Cottage, left; the White House, Mill Common now (Sandlands) centre.

*thereabouts, then and there lying Dead Upon the Oath of John Cole John Gooding Abraham Garrett Joseph Wade George Taylor John Minter John Wardley Robert King Robert Daniels Robert Aldous John ?? Matthew Mack Robert Brightwell Friday Wade and William Tebenham Good and Lawful Men …. to inquire ….. when where and how and in what manner the said Daniel Sawyer came to his Death and upon their Oath say That the said Daniel Sawyer on the sixteenth day of June …. running near to a certain Wind Mill of Samuel Browning…. One of the sails …. suddenly and by accident struck and gave him….one Mortal wound or fracture upon the right side of his Head of which the said Daniel Sawyer languished and languishing did live until the seventeenth day of June…. And then and there did die. And so the Jurors upon their oath say that …. Daniel Sawyer came to his Death by accident. And further the Jurors do say that sails of the said Wind Mill….are in possession of John Sawyer of Tunstall…., and are of the value of five shillings……"*

The father's witness statement reads: *"William Sawyer of Blaxhall Miller Father of the deceased saith that he sent his son….for his sister and in coming back by the Mill which was the way home the deceased playing with other children got near the sails and was then and there knocked down….and that it happened about 3 o'clock in the afternoon of Friday the sixteenth day of June….."*. Poor little Daniel was carried by Samuel Browning to the nearby cottage of Ann Newson, where he was laid on a blanket on the kitchen floor and the doctor called. After examination and giving what help he could, Dr, Freeman said that Daniel would "surely die" which he duly did at 7.30 the following morning.

We do not know for how long Samuel Browning was our miller but it seems likely he was, from 1809, for the next 25 years or so until William Cockerell, who lived in Tunstall, became miller in the mid-1830s. The picture is slightly muddied by record

29

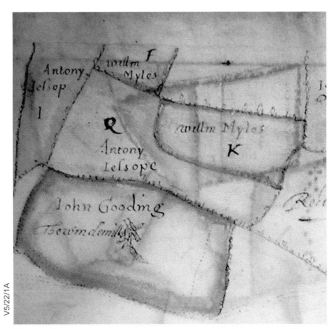

V5/22/1A

Windmills appear to come and go across the landscape. This one marked on the 1601 map by Norden must have been close to the tumulus on Blaxhall Heath.

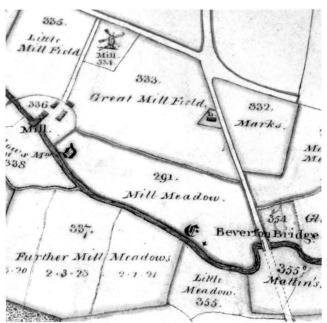

HA49/C2/4/133

The windmill marked by Kenney as 'Blaxhall 2' can be seen clearly in this map of the 1820s. The watermill at Beversham is also marked.

of a 'William Salmon of Blaxhall in the County of Suffolk, miller'. Salmon leased a watermill and a windmill from the North family at Glemhan Hall in 1818. It is likely that the windmill in question is the one referred to by Kenney as 'Blaxhall 2'.

Anyhow, after William Cockerell, who died in 1870/71, came the fateful Edward Dykes, born in Brandeston in 1845, our last miller before its destruction in 1883 - hence it is often referred to as 'Dykes Mill'.

It is not known whether the burning down of the mill was as the result of an accident/act of God or not (more of this later) but what is for sure is that windmills were dangerous places to work or play. Even with taller windmills, accidents with sails could easily occur as 'they would swing as low as a pig's back', as we have already seen, - the risk to the unwary of such a rapid moving almost silent assailant resulted in many a fatality; such as the one that occurred at Brandeston when in 1888, the unfortunate James Dykes(brother of Edward of the recently burnt Blaxhall Mill) *"was struck and killed as he stepped from the roundhouse loading door onto a load of corn on a cart....the late Mr. Hart of Framsden remarked that Dykes had 'the sails painted red and they drew red out of him'."* Clothes catching in gears was another hazard; the Ipswich Journal, May 1830, refers to an accident to Mr. Wigg, a former Tunstall miller, who caught his coat in the machinery which "drew his arm in, necessitating amputation".

If threats to life and limb were ever present, those which could damage or destroy the mill's

structure, and its owner's fortunes in the years before insurance cover became available, were no less real. Wind – gales or sudden gusts – could cause havoc with the massive oak posts being snapped or the body itself simply being blown over; a particular danger was being "tail-winded", a situation which could arise when, immediately after the wind had died away, it suddenly freshened from the opposite direction – the flyer could not respond to a wind dead on its tail, so the miller had to re-act very quickly to turn the mill round by hand to face the wind again. Lightning strikes were another serious danger, particularly as windmills were tall and there were no trees in the immediate vicinity to allow free access to the wind from any direction.

Fires were another potential cause of disaster. George Ewart Evans in his conversation with Jesse Wightman mentioned that he used to live in Blaxhall and in this connection asked why so many mills had been burnt down: *"You know that when a mill is turning, the stones have to be fed with corn all the time. If the runner stone revolves on the bed stone with nothing in between to grind there's soon trouble because the stones get hot and sparks fly out; and there is no lack in a mill of something to catch fire very quickly ... many fires started this way but many too were caused by over-heating of the jail-neck .. But sometimes there was another reason for a fire. When there was the change-over from windmills to steam-driven and later oil, many of the old windmills couldn't compete. Somehow or other a convenient fire was reckoned to be arranged".*

Millstone fragments gathered from the mill site appear to indicate that the millstones were of the largest (5ft) size.

The building that was once the mill's granary was converted to two storeys very soon after the mill's demise.

So, the miller's trade was a hard one, not without danger to life and limb as well as to his source of income; indeed, it was not uncommon for millers to go bankrupt through bad management or bad luck. As already mentioned, the availability of insurance cover from about the middle of the 19th century meant that to a large degree, he could, if prudent, be protected from financial ruin were his business to be accidentally damaged or destroyed. The advent of steam power, oil engines and roller-mills towards the end of the century meant that there was a rapid decline in the number of windmills and the millwright (whose trade was building mills and carrying out major overhauls) was being called on increasingly to demolish them. To add to the obsolescence of wind powered milling, farming was in crisis by the 1880s; cheap corn was beginning to be imported from America and the agricultural depression was affecting the fortunes of all connected with the industry. It was 'the coming down time', as the farmers called it, with profits almost non-existent and wages a pittance. Furthermore, as George Ewart Evans pointed out in his chapter on 'The Revolution in Farming' "Black '79" produced one of the worst harvests of the century, followed by a succession of wet seasons and the dreadful winter of 1880/81, one of the severest ever known; that year grain did not mature properly, mould and ergot (a disease of grasses) thrived. Not a good time then for farmers – nor for millers! In all these circumstances it must have been tempting to the unscrupulous whose business might be in trouble, to 'arrange' an accident to his mill, 'fire' being the obvious one.

According to the Gazetteer in Mr. Flint's book, over 30 mills were known to have been demolished in the last third of the 19th century, whilst in the same period only 11 are recorded as 'burnt', whether accidentally or not is unstated. Of these 11, one was the mill at Brandeston in 1893 (where our miller's brother James had been killed five years

Although many images have come to light during this project, a picture of Blaxhall Mill has eluded us. George Thomas Rope lived nearby and it is possble he drew or painted the mill. These sketches from one of his notebooks are of smock mills, so they are not Blaxhall's post mill.

earlier) and one was the great post mill in Blaxhall which *"caught fire and was destroyed after tea-time on Thursday 25th January 1883. Subsequently the stairs, fantail ('flyer') and wind tackle were put on Peasenhall mill; the tramway went to Brandeston as previously mentioned"*. Edward Dykes gave up the miller's life after the burning, left Blaxhall and apparently set up as a baker in Halesworth.

So, in the dark on that fateful January evening in 1883, the miller either must have shown great presence of mind and have acted with considerable speed and courage to save such valuable items from the conflagration, or, was the business failing and was the property insured for a tempting sum? Was it mishap or misdeed? Hearsay – direct from grandfather who lived in the converted granary from 1892, to father born 1884 to son who still lives in the old granary – strongly suggests the latter. Who knows and where is that elusive picture of the colossus of Mill Common?

*(Note: The speculation in the last paragraph is the writer's, not Mr Flint's).*

## STONE COMMON

View of Stone Common with the new Cherry Tree Cottage being built, c.1970s.

The shop, Waterloo House, on Stone Common, c.1960s.

Old Cherry Tree Cottage, c.1950s.

'The Bungalow', Stone Common, c.1970s.

## MILL COMMON

Part of Mill Common showing the Old Schoolhouse, c.1900s.

Old Post Office, Mill Common, c.1950s.

The Thatched Cottage on Mill Common, c.1900s.

The Green opposite the Ship pub, c.1950s.

Tunstall Road, c.1950s.

## OTHER PLACES IN BLAXHALL

The Forge with Church Farm (thatched) and the Village Hall in the distance, c. 1960s.

The White House on Station Road, c.1938.

Mount Pleasant on Station Road, c.1950s.

Vine Cottage in Church Road, c. 1950s.

Church Road also known as Top Road, c.1950s.

# CHAPTER ONE
# PEOPLE AND PLACES

## Part 3 - Where the people shopped

Before the age of superstores and motor cars most villages were self-contained entities, supplying much of their needs from within the parish. They had their own blacksmiths, wheelwrights, cobblers, tailors and shops that supplied all the villagers' requirements.

Blaxhall was no exception to this rule, by the mid 19th century it boasted: two blacksmiths, one wheelwright, two cobblers, two tailors and at least four shops that were either drapers, grocers or greengrocers or a mix of all of these. Added to these were itinerant salesmen who had a base in Blaxhall but would go out on a circuit around the countryside selling their wares.

There had probably been shops of one sort or another, in the village, for several centuries but the first reference we have found is in 1744. In the November Court sessions for that year is the confession of one John Wyard of Blaxhall, Butcher. He confessed that he rode one night to neighbouring Farnham and from a sheepfold belonging to Francis Osborne, spinster .."*took and stole thereout one ffat ewe*", which he carried back to Blaxhall, then killed and dressed the following day.

However, the locals seemed to know just where to look so retribution was swift to follow. The following day the aggrieved spinster, along with the constable of the parish, went to the house (and shop) of John Wyard, where they found the carcass of the stolen ewe plus the skin which showed the unique brand marks that were Francis Osborne's! There is no record of what happened to John Wyard but there is a reference to his wife and family applying for poor relief a few years later. Perhaps he was visiting Van Diemen's Land?

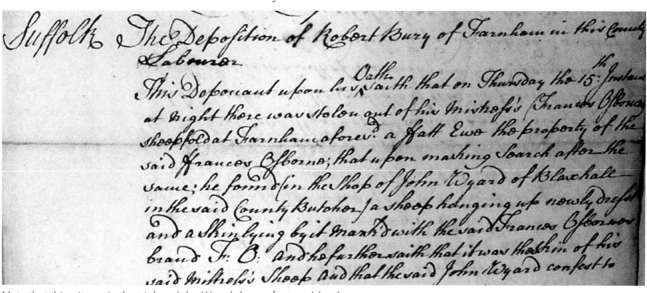

Note that this witness in the trial on John Wyard does refer to a 'shop'.

All our Blaxhall shops have a history which require our further study. However, for the Stone Common shop we have been lucky to have the memories of Mannalls and Taylors living today and also Ray Whitehand has researched his ancestors and has kindly allowed us to 'cherry pick' from his research. This means we have a fairly comprehensive history of at least one Blaxhall shop.

## The Stone Common shop

When Stone Common first had a shop, again, we are not sure – possibly there was one there in the late 18th century but our first reference is in 1823 when William Whitehand is recorded as owning the shop.

William's forebears lived mainly in the parishes around Ipswich docks and worked in various trades including cordwainers, shoemakers and retailers. William married Francis Ling in 1823 and probably moved very soon afterwards to Stone Common, as we have records of him supplying the Poor House with provisions in that year.

He styled himself as 'grocer and draper' and sold everything from sheeting, pots and pans to butter and fresh provisions. During the 1830s and 40s, as we describe earlier in this chapter, the Blaxhall population was expanding fast and William was in a position to benefit from this, not only from increased sales in his shop but also by going into real estate. It appears he built or allowed to be built three or four cottages on what was his plot of land behind the shop and house.

William relinquished the shop around 1863 but continued to live locally until his death in 1868. At this point the line of succession as regards to shopkeepers is a little grey but it seems a William Minter took over the shop. That he ran it himself in the early days is a possibility but by the 1900s a Minter, either the same individual or a relation, was known to have shops at Wickham Market, Charsfield and Debenham where the shop was also called Waterloo House.

Minter put managers into his shops and the next arrival in the shop is George Mannall who is recorded as 'manager' in 1881. George was born in Suffolk in 1849 and married Jane Ling who had been running Minter's shop in Charsfield. They both moved to Blaxhall in 1880 and brought with them two young children, George and Reginald. A third, Ada was born on Stone Common in 1881 – Ada has a whole chapter to herself later in this book.

The period from the 1880s was surely the heyday of the village shop and George presided over a prospering business. He sold everything you could call general provisions like butter, sugar, fresh, dried and canned foods as well as pots, pans, cutlery and crockery. They also sold boots, shoes, sheeting, lace and clothes and were a general outfitters with a fitting room upstairs.

At some point the Mannalls must have bought the freehold from Minter and this they finally sold on in 1917 and moved to Ipswich after nearly forty years on Stone Common.

Next came Tom Gaze and his wife who ran the shop in the same tradition of selling everything, plus a new addition which was a taxi service to the local railway station by automobile. Their stay was the shortest and they handed over to Charles and Catherine Taylor in 1932.

The Gazes in Waterloo House, c.1920s.

Charles and Catherine came from Norfolk to run the shop and they continued many of the same sale items, though there were some changes. The shoes and other haberdashery items were discontinued along with pots and pans and other ironmongery. They were long days – 8.00am until 6.00pm and closed half-day Tuesday and of course, all day Sunday. Young Ted Taylor took on the shop with his mother after 1953 and finally with his wife Carrie. Ted remembers that some items arrived in bulk like butter, which had to be cut up and wrapped into separate blocks ready for sale. A new addition during the period was an ice cream freezer!

The shop continued to serve the local inhabitants for many years trying to survive against the changing shopping habits of the 1960s and 70s. The inevitability that is called 'progress' meant it finally closed in 1979.

Shopkeeper Frank Reeve and his wife Eleanor ran his grocer's shop on Mill Common for 32 years. Here the Jackson family relax in front of Frank's shop window, c.1960s. Frank retired in 1983.

Sheila Scopes (née Shaw) outside the old Post Office, late 1950s; it had been the Post Office since the 1850s. Maurice Shaw ran it with his wife Annie (née Knights) for many years until his death in 1940, after which Annie, helped latterly by grand daughter Sheila, ran it until it closed in 1961, when it was relocated further along the Tunstall Road to Alf Brewster's shop.

Alf Brewster ran a grocery shop at Ship Cottages from 1953 until 1972. His daughter Eileen then took the business over, running the grocery side until it closed in 1991 and the Post Office until it closed in 1998. Here Eileen serves Ray Poacher and his wife Kathleen.

Various itinerant salesmen would visit cottages and sell everything from paraffin to fresh vegetables. Aldeman Ling (ABOVE) with his basket of fresh vegetables would sell to other households in the village.

(LEFT) Hawkers such as Jimmy Smy and Bob Wardley came round regularly in their horse and carts with chamber pots and nails hanging from its sides, selling households wares.

## LOST PLACES IN BLAXHALL - PUMP SQUARE

There are some houses that have completely disappeared, for example, Pump Square. Today, the site is just a cleared piece of open land adjacent the Blaxhall village sign on the left as you come from Snape. In the photograph below left Vera is sitting on a wall that would have run parallel with the road; there were six semi-detached houses on this site which were demolished in the late 1960s.

Left to right: Ivan Barker, Charlie Barker and Sylvia by the pump at Pump Square, 1951.

Mrs Vera Brown (née Hines), Pump Square c. 1960

## CHURCH ROAD

This old photograph c. 1900 has written on the back "Mrs Bates old cottage about 20 years ago before it was reconstructed". Our research tends to lead us to the conclusion that this cottage was replaced by the terrace of cottages shown on page 34 bottom right. This photograph is Oscar Ling (right) and Dan or Darcher Poacher (left).

# CHAPTER TWO
# FARMING THE LAND

## Part 1 - Farms and farmers

At the close of the Second World War there were six principal farms (Blaxhall Hall, Grove, Stone, Lime Tree, Fir Tree and Red House) operating in Blaxhall and all ran a mixed economy of pasture and arable. All these farms had their own dairy herds in 1947 and these were as important a part of each farm's income as was the arable side.

The layout of the farmsteads with their accompanying farm buildings had remained almost unaltered since the 1850s. In 1941 a government census[1] of all the Blaxhall farms recorded that there was no electricity laid on to any of the farmsteads, and that the only water supply was by well to the house and buildings and either by pond, ditch, river or water bowser to the fields. Each farm had one Fordson tractor of about 27hp. and there were 56 working horses divided between the five farms and three smallholdings in the parish.

A farm sale at Stone Farm in October 1945 included 14 Suffolk horses, a dairy herd of 82 shorthorns, dairy equipment and two nearly new Fordson tractors and a RSLD No.9 two-furrow plough, very much a picture of a mixed farming economy.

The farming depression which had lasted almost continuously from the 1870s, with only two intervals of stimulus created by two world wars, might well have returned after 1945, so government action was essential.

Lime Tree Farm, 1932 - stackyard on left and the house to the right.

Amongst the measures of social reform introduced by Attlee's Labour government immediately after the Second World War was the Agriculture Act of 1947. As well as other provisions, this guaranteed prices and markets for produce, with the aim of ensuring the more efficient use of Britain's agricultural land. Annual price reviews were instigated and prices fixed for the main crops (wheat, barley, oats, potatoes and sugar beet) for 18 months ahead. Minimum prices for fatstock, milk and eggs were fixed for between two and four years ahead.

Given stability in prices and guarantees, farm incomes rose, giving farmers the confidence to undertake capital investments and utilise the latest technology. This was especially true of arable farming: cereal prices increased at a quicker rate than other commodities; crop yields improved due to higher yielding varieties, herbicides and fertiliser; labour use and costs were reduced as the level of mechanisation increased. Whereas increases in incomes on dairy, upland and small farms were slower with less scope for mechanisation.

Even with guaranteed prices and renewed confidence in farming, the situation did not change dramatically for the next ten or fifteen years.

# Richard Rope (Grove Farm), born 1926

Richard started work in 1952 on the family farms of Lower and Upper Abbey, Leiston. At their greatest extent they jointly, covered about 1000 acres divided almost equally into pasture and arable.

A variety of livestock was kept: some sheep (which were often folded on the light arable land, to fertilise and enrich the poor soil); also a dozen breeding sows were housed, whose offspring would be taken through to bacon weight; a dairy herd of shorthorns (1952) grazed the lowland grazing marshes. These were augmented with the farm's own bullock stock and any cows not required as replacements for the dairy herd. During the short summer season animals from other farms were also taken in to feed and fatten on the lush summer growth. The cattle came off the marshes and back to the yards anytime between October and Christmas. Depending on the softness of the soil animals would not go back again to the marshes before late April or May.

The milk, from the dairy herd was taken away in churns (which continued until the 1960s), by a local dairy in Aldeburgh.

Grove Farm, c.1905, the thatched stable on the left was destroyed by fire along with many other outbuildings in May 1976.

Red House farmhouse, c. 1940.

Richard became more involved in the running of Grove Farm, Blaxhall during the 1960s and 1970s and at that time the farm consisted of 120 acres of arable and 60 acres of grass. A small dairy herd of about 20 to 25 animals was kept. The arable land either produced fodder crop for the animals, mainly kale and maize plus hay for winter feed. Some barley was grown for resale plus a quota of sugar beet. The beet was usually trucked directly to the Ipswich beet factory. Richard remembers one time when his father had a railway truck put in a siding at Snape junction and the Grove Farm beet harvest was taken and loaded there.

The 18th century thatched barn was used to store corn in sacks during the 1950s and later two portable silos within the building served the same purpose. During a fire in 1974 this barn and other outbuildings were destroyed and in their place Richard created a modern covered cattle yard and a series of storage barns.

## Raymond Herring (Red House Farm), born 1954.

Raymond's father, John Herring, in partnership with Wilfred Peek, took over the tenancy of Red House farm in 1948. At that time the farm extended to 240 acres of light, sandy soils with no artificial irrigation. The farm ran a mixed economy including a variety of livestock, beef cattle, a dairy herd, pigs and chickens, and an arable side, fodder for the animals was grown plus barley and wheat. The 1950s were a successful decade for the two partners – two new tractors were cash purchased in 1953 and a Silver Trailer Claas combine harvester was added by the mid-50s. There were eight or nine men working on the farm at this date. Irrigation was added at Red House in 1961 and this venture expanded the choice of crops that could be grown on the farm. Sugar beet, for example, would produce improved yields with the aid of irrigation, so the opportunity was taken to increase the farm's quota of this crop.

ABOVE: Church Farm (right) and the Forge, c. 1954. The thatch on Church Farm caught fire in April 1982 and the building was completely destroyed.

Raymond joined his father in 1973 after agricultural college. Just prior to this, several tenancies on nearby farms had been taken up by John, these consisted of: Street Farm, Tunstall in 1969, then Fir Tree Farm, Blaxhall in 1971 and in 1973 Plunkett's Farm, Tunstall. Together the enterprise now covered 700 to 800 acres. During the 1970s arable crops gained in importance, and whilst the chickens and pigs were phased out, there was then a move to specialising in arable and dairy. The herd consisted of commercial Friesian stock whilst a beef herd was still run at Fir Tree Farm with a choice of markets outlets at Campsey Ash, Saxmundham, Bury St. Edmunds and Ipswich.

In the early 1980s an EU-financed initiative to encourage farmers to leave milk production was taken up by Red House Farm. This created a major change in farming strategy: fields that previously were grass for grazing or grew fodder for the animals were now converted to cereal and sugar beet production and the farm became a totally arable enterprise. Larger four-wheel drive tractors and five-furrow ploughs were purchased to manage the larger arable area more efficiently.

FAR RIGHT: Glebe Farm in the 1950s.
NEAR RIGHT: Church Farm in 1936.

Blaxhall Hall farmhouse, 1936.

Stone Farm farmhouse, c. 1908.

# CHAPTER TWO

# FARMING THE LAND

## Part 2 - Some of the Fellows who Cut the Hay

Working on the land always was the principal means of employment for most of the residents of Blaxhall. As we saw in Chapter 1 up to 90% of the population in 1901 worked on the local farms and by 1950 the figure was still around 70%. But times were changing and it would be a different future for the young people who started their working lives in the late 1940s and early 1950s. They were to experience the effects of a second agricultural revolution which brought with it such innovations as the efficient use of fertilisers and herbicides and also the increasing mechanisation of all agricultural processes, including the introduction of the tractor and more importantly the arrival of the combine harvester.

## Terry Skeet, born 1936.

Terry started work for Robert Sherwood at Lime Tree Farm in 1951. Mr Sherwood was a good employer but young Terry wanted to make it clear from the outset that he didn't want to start as the 'back'us boy'. This was usually the newest and youngest member of the farming team whose chores could include feeding chickens, chopping sticks, plucking pheasants or any other indoor job the farmer might require. So Terry did not start as the back'us boy but had an outdoor assignment – six weeks of scaring rooks off the fields with only the aid of his own voice to encourage the birds to fly .

Working at Lime Tree around this time (1951) besides the 14 men were six Suffolk Punches with names like Duke, Bessie, Tedder, Bellamy and Bowler, and three tractors including an old Ford Major which had to be started with a crank handle.

As a young man he was invited to work with the horses and this included many tasks like carting sugar beet tops to the fields as a supplementary feed for the cows.

At harvest time there were three wagons (carts) each drawn by a single horse, engaged in a rotation of removing the cut harvest from the field to the stackyard. Terry explained how it worked; "One cart was in the field loading, another cart was at the stack off loading and the third cart was on its way back to the field".

Building a haystack was a skilled job and experienced men were getting hard to find by the 1950s. Robert Sherwood employed Aldeman Ling to do this job. A man already in his forties, 'Aldie' was a good stackman and, if young Terry could draw his loaded wagon right up close to the half-built stack, then it would save the stackman a lot of work. Aldie would throw a penny down to Terry every time "he drawed up right close to the stack".

Stack building on Mill Walk, Lime Tree Farm, 17 June 1931.

The farm pond at Lime Tree Farm, August 1934, used to refuel both horses and cows alike.

Aldie came into work one day with a tale. He said to young Terry, "I'm not drinking tea no more, boy". Terry asked "Why's that, Aldie?" "Well" he says, "for sometime our kettle not been pouring too well, so I decided to set to with a piece of wire to clear the spout, only to pull out the skeleton of a mouse!" Not surprisingly, tea didn't have quite the same taste after that.

Another job was to take the water out to the cows in the fields. This was in the days, around 1963, before water was piped to standing pipes in the fields. The horse was harnessed to the water cart and both horse and cart were backed into the farm pond until the cart was filled with 80 to 90 gallons of water.

Reaper binder at work on Backhouse Field, Lime Tree Farm, 17 August 1931.

Bob Sherwood (right) farmed Lime Tree Farm, Blaxhall from the 1920s until the mid-1960s.

Walter Skeet at Lime Tree with one of the farm's prize shorthorns, c.1943.

Lime Tree Farm c. 1940.

Stone Farm cowmen. Left to right: Robert French, George Smith and Dank Scarce.

George 'Nature' Reeve.

Harvest 1952. Left to right: Tom Jay, Ray Poacher, Marji Reeve, Terry Dunnett and George Reeve.

Lime Tree Farm c.1910. Centre is James Stebbing with his son George on the left.

# John Gant, born 1935.

John was in agriculture all his working life. First starting at Dunningworth Hall in 1950, then a short spell at Foxhall, outside Ipswich, from which he returned to work as a tractor driver at Stone Farm, Blaxhall in 1960.

In 1950, nine men worked at Dunningworth Hall, which was a farm of approximately 300 acres in size and divided almost half and half, arable and grazing. These wet grassland meadows stretched from Iken along the southern shore of the Alde, past the Maltings, then on upriver to Langham. John's first job was to cut kale to feed to the dairy herd. He remembers that the kale was as high as he was and although dressed in waterproof jacket and leggings, he was wet through after only half an hour's work. After a few weeks of this, he also got the job of carting this fodder to the marshes as feed for the cattle. The farm's marshes below Snape Bridge were also used for hay. The Great Flood of 1953 broke through the river wall and flooded all the low lying area. Although the breach was repaired and the marshes drained, the same thing occurred again some years later and they now remain part of the picturesque scene of mudflats and reedbeds around the Snape Maltings Concert Hall. At low tide you can still see the old gateposts, the only reminder of the areas earlier usage.

In 1960 John and his young wife Daphne, were lured to Blaxhall from Foxhall by the enticement of a larger cottage with indoor toilet, electricity and tapped indoor running water (cold only, of course!). John now worked for Robin Graham who farmed Stone Farm in Blaxhall as well as Chantry Farm, Campsey Ash. Stone Farm in 1960 was about 200 acres in extent, divided again, half arable and half pasture. Five men worked on the farm, there were two cowmen and two tractor drivers of which John was one. His tractor was a four-cylinder Fordson Diesel, two not four-wheel drive as most tractors were at that time but quite adequate for all the jobs it was asked to do. However, just occasionally in an area of difficult land, two machines (one behind the other), would be needed to work the plough.

The Fordson was capable of ploughing five acres in a day, and there were a hundred or so arable acres on the farm but there was a longer period after harvest for ploughing and preparing fields for the new crop. Few autumn sown crops were planted as most were spring sown. So as John says, "you could plough past Christmas into January and February".

Steam power at Blaxhall, c.1905.

.. "YOU COULD PLOUGH
PAST CHRISTMAS INTO
JANUARY AND FEBRUARY".

Lime Tree Farm, c.1930.

## Ray Poacher, born 1928.

This photograph of a rye stack was taken by Ray Poacher down at Blaxhall Hall Farm during the summer of 1960. On a part time basis Ray would help Fred Pearce thatch the stacks as they were completed.

The stacks were built by the horsemen of the farm and they would ask Fred to come and thatch it – preferably before it rained. Ray explains what came next, "They would draw a cart of wheat straw up against the stack. It was long straw cut by a binder, not cut like it is today by a combine. They would then bring up a water cart and I would chuck water all over the straw and 'shak' it up. It would work better wet both for me sorting it in bundles and for Fred when he laid it and combed it on the top of the stack".

Ray sorted the straw into bundles, making sure it all ran the same way and getting rid of any rubbish. Eight or ten of these straw bundles were

A completed rye stack. Fred Pearce's final touch was to trim around the eaves of the thatch with a pair of sheep shears to create a trim and tidy appearance.

Playing in the haystacks was a childhood game for those fortunate enough to live in the country. These are Bob Sherwood's children at Lime Tree Farm during the 1930s.

fitted into the yoke. The yoke was a V-shaped piece of equipment made of 'nuttery wood' (hazel) and was the tool that held the bundles firm and allowed Ray to carry them up the stack ladder to Fred. The stack ladder was upwards of 30 feet in height (39 staves or rungs) and was the largest and heaviest ladder on the farm. Being right-handed Fred started laying the straw bundles from the left, making sure as he did, that they all ran the same way. When firm and in place, a comb with his thatching rake achieved the waterproof qualities to the thatch. All was held in place by a row of broaches – straight ones (18" long) were used for thatching. These broaches were spliced and when pushed into the thatch held down a string that ran the whole length of the stack; about six rows of broaches and string were used on each side of the stack. This technique protected the thatch from the high winds.

The last job was to measure up the stack with the use of a long tape which was thrown over the stack and the measurement taken. Thatching was paid for by the square yard.

Esau Ling (left), Ben Ling (centre) and David 'Nipper' Ling on their smallholding situated behind the school, early 1920s.

Blaxhall plough teams, c.1900s, possibly Stone Farm. Left to right the little boy on the second team of horses is Wally Hammond, next to him George Hammond. On the right of the third horse team with the white beard, Harry Basket.

## Roderick Hammond, born 1960.

Roderick joined the workforce at Red House Farm as a young teenager in 1976. His first chores were to help look after the cattle. Farmer John Herring had both a milking herd which was kept at Red House Farm and a beef herd at Fir Tree Farm, which the family were also running at this date. The 120-head milking herd was kept in yards at Red House and let out,when the weather permitted, onto the marshes between morning and evening milkings.

In 1982 the milk herd was sold off and Roderick moved onto larger tractors, using for ploughing, for example, a Ford 8200 four-wheel drive tractor with a Ransomes four-furrow reversible plough. Today (2006) he is using a Ford TM150 with a five furrow reversible plough. Depending on weather and soil conditions he would have expected to plough 10 to 15 acres a day in 1982 and 15 to 20 or more acres in a day today (2006). Roderick says

that, "Sitting in a tractor today is like sitting in your own front room – with ergonomically designed seating, air-conditioning, radio and CD player all fitted as standard and GPS equipment additional if required".

In 1976 the Herring family were running 700-800 acres with 11 men, each with a tractor; no working horses were left on the farm by this date. In 2006, Raymond Herring is running a similar acreage but with just himself and Roderick as the workforce. Weather conditions, obviously, still affect the harvest but generally the harvest begins mid to late July with rape and barley being the first crops, then followed by wheat. Roderick would expect to harvest these crops from the present 700 acres in about three weeks, then be ready to sow the majority of the next season's crops in September – most being in before Christmas. In a wet winter some spring wheat and spring rape would be sown in the spring.

Harvest 2005. Roderick Hammond makes adjustments to the combine.

# Mary Smith (née Price) born 1922.

Mary was born on Stone Common, Blaxhall and lived there until she married. As a young woman she worked from 1941 at Plunkett's Farm just over the parish border in Tunstall; she would walk or bicycle there each day. One of her jobs was to help the farmer's wife, Mrs Reynolds, make butter and cheese.

This is how Mary explained the making of butter in an age when there was no running water or electricity. First the fresh milk of the day was put through the cooler and left to settle in a large bowl. The cream would then rise to the top and was 'creamed off' with a ladle. This all went into a large wooden barrel churn and Mary would begin to turn the handle – which went for some time! "You know when it was ready when it started lumping", said Mary. The whey had separated from the butter fats and was drained off to a bucket and fed to the pigs.

The butter was placed on a slab and then piece by piece was pressed into either a butter mould with a decorative motif and pressed out into circular shapes; or using butter pats, the butter was formed into either rectangles or circular portions. These were then wrapped in greaseproof paper and kept on cold slate slabs in the dairy. They were sold to anyone who wanted to buy some.

Soft cheese was also made – the milk was "left to rest" in a large bowl, then rennet was added and the curdled mix was laid into round tins. These tinned young cheeses were laid onto straw mats and allowed to settle and drain. A delicious creamy cheese is the result according to Mary!

Another job was to prepare the milk consignment for the local school. The order came over first thing in the morning and milk from the morning's milking was used to fill the third of a pint-size bottles. Cardboard lids were fastened down with a special tool and the crates were delivered to the school in time for break. The empty bottles were returned at the end of the school day, to be scalded clean and ready for the next day's order.

Fred Mayhew ran a local milk round - here he is seen delivering to the cottages on Stone Common.

George Smith with his master's flock c.1900. He moved from Blaxhall to Church Farm, Aldeburgh where he died of pneumonia at the early age of 46.

# CHAPTER THREE
# THE LADY BEHIND THE LENS

During this community project we have collected many hundreds of photographs illustrating the social life of Blaxhall. Occasionally, a photograph would arrive with the signature 'A. Mannall' written on a corner. These photographs were always beautifully composed, inevitably of a very interesting subject and of superb quality. They appeared to date from the first two decades of the twentieth century.

Who was 'A. Mannall'? With some research and the kind help and assistance of Reg and Ada Mannall, (nephew and niece of Ada), the mysterious signature had become a real person – and what a treasure!

Ada Mannall was born at Waterloo House, Stone Common, Blaxhall in 1881. She was the youngest of three children; George and Reginald were her two older brothers. Brother George married Alice Matilda Ling who are the parents of the present Reg and Ada.

Ada's father, George Mannall, and mother Jane, née Stollery, ran the shop at Stone Common from the early 1880s until 1917 when they moved to Ipswich. Ada went to Blaxhall School, and then worked for Cowells the printers in Ipswich where she lived with her parents in Bartholomew Street.

Ada's interest in photography appears to have started in her twenties when she acquired a half-plate camera, at which point she started out on a quest of photographing both people and places not only in Blaxhall but also further afield. She obviously had a 'good eye' for a picture as you will see from the examples in this chapter. Those of Blaxhall appear to date from about 1902 until 1917. A number are in postcard format, which Ada produced herself and signed and annotated in what appears to have been originally gold ink,

perhaps she sold them in Stone Common shop.

Many of the photographs are of Grove Farm, Blaxhall either of people there or agricultural operations. One wonders if she had a friendship with some of the young, artistic women who lived or stayed there like Ellen Mary Rope, Margaret Agnes Rope and Margaret Edith Rope, all of whom would have been her contemporaries.

Ada at St. Bartholomew Street, Ipswich c.1930s.

Jane Mannall, c.1920s

George Mannall, c. 1920s.

Jane and George Mannall with children Reginald (left), George (centre) and Ada (right).

We originally thought that Ada had started taking photographs around 1902 but some detective work by Reg Mannall has found an Ada Mannall photograph of an intact Rendlesham Hall, which was largely destroyed by fire on 9 May 1898. By inference this means that Ada took this photograph before that date, when she was 17 years old or younger.

RIGHT: Scouts at Rendlesham Hall
BELOW RIGHT: Ada with Kitty the pony.
LEFT: George Mannall on Stone Common with the present Reg and Ada as children.
BELOW LEFT: New shoes for Kitty at Tunstall smithy (behind the Green man pub) with George Mannall in the background, c.1905.

Hoeing potatoes on 'Funny Hill' with Stone Common in the distance. Ada had taken three studies of these particular ladies; shown here are one and two in the series, c. 1905.

The same ladies, taking a break: from the left, Lizzie Baskett, Ann Jay, Eliza Reeve and Lizzie Ling.

Mowing at Blaxhall, c. 1910

Suffolk & Essex Yeomanry at Rendlesham Hall, c. 1906.

Old Farm, Blaxhall, now known as Old Barn Cottages, c. 1910.

Mill Common, Blaxhall, c. 1910

A rear view of the Mount Pleasant row of cottages, c.1910.

Rear view of Acorn Cottage, Blaxhall, c.1902

Floods at Blaxhall.

View from Langham Bridge of the floods in the meadows of Fir Tree Farm, August 27, 1912.

The Garden, Blaxhall Hall

The gardens at Blaxhall Hall, c. 1910

Sheep on Funny Hill, Stone Common, c. 1910

Fir Tree Farm, Blaxhall, c.1910

One of Ada's postcards showing reaping at Blaxhall Hall Farm, c.1905

Ploughing match at Blaxhall, 16 June 1909. Record entries of 152 men and 33 boys.

A winter scene, probably the meadows by Fir Tree Farm, c.1912

Reapers at work, Blaxhall; note Mount Pleasant cottages in the distance, c.1910,

Sheep shearing at Grove Farm, Blaxhall, c. 1910

Ada on Pound Walk, Stone Common, Blaxhall, c. 1902.

George Mannall at about 18 years old, in the churchyard at Blaxhall, c. 1902

George Mannall with young Reg, outside Cherry Tree Cottage, Stone Common, Blaxhall, c. 1926.

'Old' George Rope in his garden at Grove Farm, c. 1904

The gardens at Blaxhall Hall, c.1912.

Meet of the Oakley Hounds at Blaxhall Hall, March 10 1911.

Two images of Beversham Water Mill. The motive power was probably not the water wheel by this date but a diesel engine. When Ada took these photographs around 1910, it was still a working mill. Ada had referenced the negatives as 'Stannard's Mill', the name of the then owner.

Beech Grove, Blaxhall.

From a series of four negatives showing the sequence of timber being loaded onto a timber 'jim'. This is the last image.

The gatekeeper's cottage at Beversham crossing.

Repairs on the line, c. 1910. Ada seems to have been able to get all the workers to stand still for a few seconds!

A snow-covered Stone Common, c. 1910.

Delivering the post at Stone Common, c. 1904.

Glebe Farm, Blaxhall, c.1905.

Church Cottages in need of a new thatch, c.1905.

Blaxhall Church from the north-east c. 1905.

Langham Bridge, c.1910.

Beversham Bridge, c.1910.

Children standing on what is now the A12 at Little Glemham, with the turning to Blaxhall in the distance on the right, c.1910.

A field of saffron at Little Glemham, c.1910.

# CHAPTER FOUR
# VILLAGE FUN AND GAMES

Those of us too young to know any better are often told by our elders that.. "we made our own entertainment in those days". We nod in agreement not knowing really what they meant. But after looking at this chapter of photographs, the community entertainment to which they were referring becomes very clear. And remember, these photographs are just the scenes that were recorded on film, add to them: the Women's Institute; the Blaxhall Library; the History Group; the Hand Bell Ringers; the Art Club; the Labour Club and many more. The inevitable conclusion is, surely, when looking at this vibrancy and wealth of endeavour, that these pursuits were the life blood of the community. Engaging with other parishioners helped create a 'bonding' and a sense of community which in turn produced a feeling of identity and a 'sense of place' which perhaps is now not so strong in this modern age of the car and mass media, although Blaxhall can still boast: an Art Group; a Line Dancing Club; an Indoor Bowls Club; an Environment Group; an Archive Group and a village website, that is regularly updated and contains much parish information; 'hits' to the website show that Blaxhall now has a global following.

Blaxhall residents work together to help clear leaves away from the churchyard, 2005.

## A Day Out

A day out brings back memories of warm summer days and a simple picnic in a field or a trip to Iken Cliff to go for a swim. Generations of Blaxhall children learnt to swim in the river at Langham Bridge. Upriver from the bridge was a deeper area ideal for the purpose and parties of children were taken from the school and taught to swim at Langham.

Charabanc outing, c. 1920s.

An outing to Felixstowe.

A summer picnic - this field is now the playing field adjacent to the Village Hall. This is the Baker family from the White House and friends picnicking , 1953. Note the forge and wheelwrights buildings in the background.

The Sherwood family from Lime Tree Farm setting off for a trip to Iken, sometime in the 1930s.

Blaxhall to Great Yarmouth outing around 1950.

# CYCLE SPEEDWAY

At the first bend - leading Terry Skeet and lying second Brian Davidson.

The Blaxhall Cycle Speedway Club started in about 1950, it was a popular sport with clubs all over the region. Some clubs had their tracks made for them by local councils, but the Blaxhall B's, built their own up on Blaxhall Common on an area of redundant allotment near the site known as the Gypsy Pit – the concrete starting pad is still there in the undergrowth.

The most important quality of a cycle track is that it is flat, so on the sloping land of the common the boys had to dig deep (four or five feet), in some places to create the desired flat surface. Arthur Drewery brought two loads of sugar beet sludge up to the site and this was laid all over the track and tamped down. Whilst still workable, crushed cinder was then rolled into the surface and this created an extremely durable track surface.

The Blaxhall 'B's competed in an official league with other local teams, several from Ipswich and Woodbridge (Wildcats). A team consisted of seven with two reserves. All races were adjudicated by trained referees – local farmer Robin Graham was one of those who took on the role with relish. He also would send a water bowser from the farm to damp down the track in dry weather.

At its height the Blaxhall club had upwards of 20 riders aged between 12 and 18 years, some a little older. The club carried on until the late 1950s.

The start of the cycle speedway track on Blaxhall Common near Gypsy Pit. The starting tapes were a good idea but unfortunately did not work properly. Kenny French is far right and presumably was acting as starter. For the 'B's - far left: Ted Coe, third from left George Brown.

At the third bend - Ted Coe lies third with Henry Keeble close on the outside.

At the start of the cycle speedway event.

# THE RECTORY

Blaxhall Fete at the Rectory. Left to right: Maud Skeet, The Reverend Browne, Elizabeth Ling and Rachel Cowley.

Speech giving - 1953. Standing left: Albert Poacher, Frank Reeve (hidden), Mr Hare, Mr Baker, seated Mrs Baker then The Reverend Browne.

'Bowling for the Pig' - three pin bowling at the Blaxhall Fete in the Rectory Gardens - 1953. Left to right: Eileen Brewster, Valerie Brewster, unknown individual, Mr Baker, Roy Leek, Ted Coe, Peter Lee, Clive Curtis and Brian Davidson.

Garden Fete at Blaxhall Rectory, 1960. Left to right: Marion Burch, Clive Woolnough, Robert Burch, Michael Bantoft, Michael Plant (holding strings), Douglas Smith and Paul Smith.

## BLAXHALL ROVERS

The late Mr A Butcher of Tunstall took this photograph of the Rovers. They are back row left to right: Walter Ling, William Ling, Jock Hardwicke, P.L. Richardson, front row; Frank Reeve, Fred Taylor, Alfred Richardson, William Poacher and William Durrant.

### Village entertainers of long ago

People who think that village life before the days of television and radio was limited to hard work during the day and early to bed at night obviously don't know about the gaiety at Blaxhall over 50 years ago.

Those were the days of the Blaxhall Rovers Concert Party, eight young men who could sing, dance and give a good account of female impersonation – probably the first of the Suffolk Danny La Rues- generally keeping audiences well entertained for an evening.

Mr Percy Richardson of Wickham Market, was a member. Their pianist was a schoolboy, Fred Taylor, of Little Glemham.

Mr Richardson remembers, "Seven of us are still left, but scattered over the country. We performed mostly in the winter, and would begin rehearsing for the "season" in September at the home of one of our members, William Durrant, since he was the only member who could afford a piano.

This meant Fred Taylor had to cycle over from

Little Glemham to Blaxhall. Our first concert was always given at Blaxhall for whichever charity the village would name.

The programme opened with a full chorus and at least one song per member and encores if asked for. Following the interval, another fresh song would be contributed by each member".

### Model T Ford

Mr Richardson recalled that the party's transport was an old Model T Ford belonging to David Hudson of Little Glemham, and he was called in to act as chauffeur. During the day it was used to cart sand and gravel from Blaxhall pits and afterwards it was swept out and fitted with wooden forms to accommodate the party. An old army blanket would be hung over the back to keep out the cold winds. Arriving at village halls throughout the Deben area – Tunstall, Marlesford, Hasketon, Iken, Sudbourne, Orford, Knodishall, Aldeburgh, Hacheston, Snape and Bruisyard, the party would be greeted by a stream of people carrying lanterns and hurricane lamps to guide them.

Admission to the concert cost the whole audience five shillings only, (this was for the pianist) and each village provided refreshments.

Mr Richardson said each member was responsible for his own props and music. In those days, he recalled, he could buy sheet music for about sixpence unless he was lucky enough to find a comic song included in a Sunday paper, included at that time as a regular feature.

### Burnt Cork

He and his brother Alfred were the comedians; their make-up consisted of burnt cork, grease paint and a red stick marker used by the local shepherd to mark his sheep during the breeding season. Removing the make-up presented some problems. "We only had a drop of cold water when we got home, as my mother had gone to bed and the fire was out, and not all of the make-up washed off- there were always traces on the pillow case and sheets".

*Article first published Thursday March 27 1975 Mercury Series*

# Hard times at Blaxhall

Sir, — Have just received a couple of news cuttings taken from your paper, one a resume on the village of Blaxhall, one a photo and short article on the Blaxhall Rovers Concert party.

As one of those depicted in the photo (third from left, back row) I was very pleased to receive them. We worked hard to make it a success and enjoyed doing so, although sometimes we were very late home, after a journey — 1 or 2 o'clock in the morning, and some of us having to be at work at 5 a.m. it meant a quick cup of tea, a wash, change into our working clothes and off up the road to work.

But the fact that is most missed by writers is the fact that the Blaxhall concert party was formed as a result of a concert got up to make funds to help almost starving villagers. Yes, almost starving! A farm labourer's money at that time was 28 shillings per week if you were out of work — no dole, no Social Security, you went on parish relief (or the workhouse).

If a married man, parish relief might mean two days work in the stone pit at 5s. per day, 10s. for your week, and not necessarily every week. Single men might get one day per week.

Just imagine what that meant in terms of food etc. That winter was a bad one for those who depended on the sugar beet for work. So some of us got together and ran a concert to get some funds. It was a great success and we were able to give some help to those who needed it most.

The Blaxhall Rovers concert party developed from there. I am over 70 now and these pictures brought back both good and bad memories for me. My wife was a Blaxhall girl and her father, John Knights, was one of those who could dish out a punch if wanted, at the Ship Inn.

E. J. (Jock) HARDWICKE
259 Perry Street,
Billericay,
Essex.

# OTHER PURSUITS

ABOVE: During the 1930s the Blaxhall football pitch was on one of the fields belonging to Bob Sherwood at Lime Tree Farm. A pre-match pitch inspection was essential if cows had been using the field recently!

Peter Fletcher in Blaxhall black and white football strip.

Roy Edwards aged 17 in blue and white Blaxhall football strip.

BELOW: 1935 Blaxhall School football and netball teams. Left to right backrow; Alec Cable, Basil Ling, Christopher Lord (Manny), Hazel Jay, Edna Wardley, Ethel Drewery, Ivy Winter. 3rd row left to right; Donald Ling, Percy Drewery. 2nd Row seated left to right; David Savage, Jack Plant, Connie French, Poppy Hewitt, Mary Price. Front Row Left to right; Arthur Drewery, Alfie Ling, John Ling, Charlie Smith

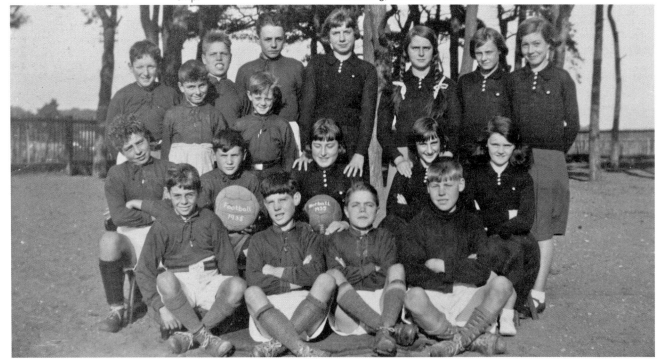

Blaxhall football team - Sunday Morning League Division Five winners - 1970/71. Back row L to R: B. Knights, R. Bantoft, D. Davies, I. Backhouse, A. Cable, M. Plant, B. Davidson (manager). Front row L to R: D. Gant, A. Rose, Colin Woolnough (captain), B. Chandler, R. Ling and D. Berry.

The Blaxhall British Legion Darts team, c.1950s  Back row left to right: Frank Reeve, Peter Jay, Chris 'Manny' Lord, Will Drewery, George Scarce, The Reverend Boorman. Seated left to right: Geoff Ling, Eli Durrant and Abie 'Young Abie' Ling.

ABOVE: Blaxhall Rifle Club, c, 1918.  BELOW: The Rifle Club members preparing the site for the Club hut. This shooting gallery was in the pit behind Lime Tree Farm

Blaxhall Girl Guides, c. 1950s. Back row Left to right: Maudie French, Pamela Cable, May Smith, Jean Richardson. Front row left to right: unknown, Pat Hammond, unknown, Dorothy Double.

Mother's Union meeting, c.1920s.

The men and women of the British Legion - Blaxhall section, march towards the Village Hall, c. 1950s.

A quiet pony ride across the countryside was just as popular 50 years ago as it is today. Karen Baker and Joanna climb 'Funny Hill' with Stone Common in the background.

Pigeon racing was another spare time pursuit, here a young Peter Edwards, when living at Acorn Cottage, gave his birds the very best accommodation!

During the 1950s the pit by the village hall was converted into a play area for the children of the village. George Ewart Evans gets help cementing an old tractor into position. This proved to be a favourite play item.

## PLAYING FIELD

Opening of the playing field by Sir Robert Gooch, Bt.

The crowds gather for the opening.

ABOVE & BELOW: A hog roast was enjoyed by the locals in the evening of the opening day.

Blaxhall folk at the village fete, 1953.

Bonfire Night - November 5th is another event celebrated on the playing field. Here Linda Keeble supervises 'sparkler' practice.

## Losing a few pounds to help raise many more

Villagers joined forces in 1996 to raise money towards the £8,000 for play equipment. Sponsored events included: a sponsored slim, a car boot sale and a cricket match.

LEFT & BELOW: The annual Fete is still held on the playing field each summer. These are scenes from a sunny, successful 2004.

THE VILLAGE HALL

ABOVE: A dinner of the Blaxhall Men's Club.

Girls from Blaxhall in Japanese dress in an event to raise funds for World War I wounded.

**From the Blaxhall & Glemham magazine :**
" *A most successful Concert was held in the Parish Room on Tuesday, February 15 1916. It was given by the children of the Blaxhall Voluntary School in aid of the Voluntary War Supply Fund. The large audience showed the interest that had been aroused. The way the children acquitted themselves showed the infinite patience and care taken in their training by Mrs Whitehead and Miss Sparrow, and the applause from time to time manifested the audience's appreciation of it.*

*The topical songs - 'Little Tommy Atkins', The Red Cross Nurses', 'The Aeroplane' and 'Kitchener's Boys' were especially applauded: whilst the 'Gay Little Girls from Japan' (in character) made a pleasing group".*

Blaxhall Youth Club used the hall for many years. in this photograph The Reverend Browne left, Walter Pipe centre.

An art exhibition is now an annual event in the village hall.

Many plays were held in the hall and performed by the Blaxhall Drama Group, c.1950s.

Father Christmas arrives at the village hall, December 2004.

'Best Hat' competition, November 5th 2001.

The village hall after 96 years of service to the residents of Blaxhall is now undergoing a major extension and refurbishment which will provide a new kitchen, toilets, entrance hall and additional rooms.

# THE SHIP INN

The Ship Inn, 1953.

The Ship Inn has been plying its trade for at least 250 years and probably longer. A map of the 1820s marks the inn and the windmill as amongst a small scatter of buildings on Mill Common. In these early days the Ship's premises were also used by the courts to hold inquests and other legal functions. Weddings and other celebrations were held here before the Parish Room was built in 1911.

From at least the early years of the 20th century folk music had been sung and danced in the pub. The heyday for folk singing in the Ship was probably during the 1950s until the 1970s during which time at least two BBC documentaries were made, many songs recorded and numerous photographs taken, some of which are shown on these pages.

Lily Durrant (née Reeve) and Eli Durrant step dancing in The Ship, c.1950s. Behind Lily can be seen Fred Pearce playing accordion and behind Eli is 'Wicketts' Richardson.

Left to right: standing 'Wicketts' Richardson, seated Lewis Poacher, Eli Durrant then Geoff Ling standing. In front of him Lilly Durrant next to Mr Church and Mary Keeble. In the front Daphne Renfro (née Hammond) and Lee.

Conga Dance at The Ship, c.1950s. In the front is Eli Durrant, second Daphne Hammond, third Fred Pearce (top of his head only), fourth Abi Ling jnr. then Arthur Drewery.

BELOW: Kathleen Poacher sings in The Ship, c.1953.

Enjoying a drink in the autumn sunshine, October, 1953. Left to right: 'Wicketts' Richardson, Lou Poacher, Frank Reeve, Will Scarce, Cyril Poacher and 'Smut' Bailey.

## QUOITS

It is not certain just when Blaxhall got its first quoits team. The team was certainly a going concern by the early 1900s as matches are frequently mentioned in the Church magazine. Peter Fletcher was in the boy's team whilst at school, which would be during the 1920s, and he remembers that most villages locally had at least one team, this included: Blaxhall, Butley, Snape, Tunstall, Leiston, Benhall, Friston, Saxmundham and Kelsale.

By the 1920s there was an official league in which teams played for two cups: the Sir Guy Hamilton Cup, which was for singles and the Rendlesham Cup for teams of three. Peter won the singles cup once, just after the Second World War.

Blaxhall had a set of permanent quoits beds in the field opposite the village hall; this field originally

held a large clay pit and it was here that the quoits beds were placed, with just the right material at hand to make the quoit bed. Other beds made by the boys were at Stone Common (on the triangle) and at Mill Common.

Matches were usually played during the long summer evenings and each team consisted of six players. During the inter-war years Blaxhall had enough players to fill two teams. By the time Peter was in the men's team other members included Fred Keeble (captain), George Scarce, Jack Ling and Jack French.

Men's quoits weighed 3.5lbs each, the boys' about half that.

Young men aspiring to being quoits players, c. 1943.
Note horseshoes made a good substitute quoit.
Left to right: Ivan Skeet, Terry Skeet, Henry Hammond
and Terry Dunnett.

ABOVE: Quoits match in progress which included Blaxhall men. BELOW: 1930's Quoits match again including Blaxhall players.
The venue could possibly be Christchurch Park in Ipswich.

# MOTOCROSS

The Blaxhall Motocross circuit has been part of the village scene for nearly fifty years. Originally named Rendlesham Motor Cycle Club it was formed in 1956 and used several venues in the area during the early years. The Blaxhall circuit became one of the club's venues in the early 1960s and was originally hired from Hall & Co. Sand & Gravel, where a Mr Ray Brooker was manager and would check after each event that the club had left the pit clean and tidy.

The club needed a pits area which was the Rectory paddock, whilst parking was in the field opposite. In 1979 BBC television visited Blaxhall circuit to film a programme in conjunction with the Sports Council called 'Sport Types'; this was broadcast on 4th December 1979. Up until this time the club would borrow part of Long Field for parking; in 1980 the opportunity came to buy half the field for car parking. Also in 1983 ARC Ltd. accepted an offer from the club to buy the gravel pit area itself. After these successful negotiations the club now had a permanent venue.

A name change occurred in 1966 to the Woodbridge & District Motor Cycle Club and a limited company was formed. Over the years the club has used the Blaxhall circuit to host many national events like the ATV National Championships and the National TMX/Talon Sidecar Cross Series and also over the same period of time many international events. The

Woodbridge & District team have won numerous trophies including, for example, the Centre Grass Track Championship Shield which they have won for the past 14 years.

In 1968 the club presented the village with a seat for villagers and this was renewed after many years of use in 2000. For many years the club also presented the Church with a Christmas tree each year.

The club is also portrayed on the village sign with a motocross bike and rider on it - probably the only sign in the country to incorporate such a feature.

All four wheels off the ground! - 2005

ABOVE: At the starting gates - 2004    BELOW: A summer scene at Blaxhall circuit, c.1960s.

# BLAXHALL ENTERTAINMENT – 2006

In 2006 the village hall, each week, provides a venue for line dancing and, below left, carpet bowls.

Regular meetings of the Blaxhall Art Club are held in the village hall, 2006.

Blaxhall residents join together to plant new hedgerow each winter season.

# CHAPTER FIVE
# ST. PETER'S HIDDEN KEYS

It is perhaps stating the obvious to say that Blaxhall Church St. Peter's is the oldest building in the parish, but what is not quite so obvious is the age of the building. The nave and chancel are probably the most ancient parts of the structure, for they contain windows (especially the east window) that experts date to c.1300. The hammerbeam roof on the other hand is dated as early 15th century, so presumably there was another earlier roof, perhaps of thatch that was replaced by this later one.

After the nave and chancel, next to be built was the tower or steeple, very much the fashionable extra in the 1400s. The present west doorway (now bricked-up) would then have been the main entrance into the Church and a very old trackway known as Holy-gate Path led directly to this doorway from the direction of Stone Farm. Over the west doorway, on the left-hand side, is a carving of an angel holding the heraldic arms of the Earls of Ufford, possibly they were the principal benefactors of the tower's construction. Experts say that the carving on the right-hand side is a 'grotesque'. but Blaxhall folk prefer to see it as a 'green man'.

The south-facing porch also dates from the 15th century. Porches played an important role in church affairs during the medieval period. For example, penitents received absolution within the porch before entering the church. Sometimes executors of wills made payments of legacies in the porch confines and also public notices were displayed there.

Any building, with over 700 years of history behind it, will record within its fabric many repairs and

alterations and Blaxhall Church is no exception. When looking at the Church today the most obvious major repair is the brickwork addition to the otherwise flint-built tower. There do not seem to be any records of this repair and when it was done, but there are some clues. For example, in 1692 there is a reference in the Ipswich Quarter Sessions which records that: *"Upon reading the petion* (sic) *of the Inhabitants of Blaxall setting forth that their parish Church is soo Ruinous that they are in great danger of harme whilst they have Divine Service there. And that*

This flint flushwork symbol is known as the Monogram of the Blessed Virgin, where the two letters MR (Maria Regina) are joined. The crown above the letters shows that Mary is Queen of Heaven.

Over the west doorway is a carving of an angel holding the arms of the Earls of Ufford.

On the right-hand side above the west doorway is a carving of a 'grotesque' or perhaps a 'green man'.

*ye charge of Reparying the Sayd Church and Steple will amount to £250 att the least..".* Their petition was successful as they got £13 back from the taxman! This plea, repeated again in the following year, indicates that not all was right with the fabric of the Church around the end of the 17th century. But by 1745 when a local antiquarian visited the Church he made this observation: *" Square stiple, decayed formerly on the upper part, but repaired with brick..".* So it looks as if these major structural problems had been sorted out by this date.

Other noticeable repairs include the brick-built windows both on the north and south side of the nave; although copying the Perpendicular style of earlier centuries, they could also date from the early 18th century repair work.

The next major refurbishment was undertaken by the enthusiastic Victorians during the 1860s, and this created more or less the Church interior we recognise today. But before listing these changes let us see if we can gain a picture of the Church interior before this major event.

An antiquarian by the name of David Elisha Davy

made several visits to the Church, the first in 1807, with further visits on and off for the next forty years. In later life he was a friend of Ellis Wade, the Blaxhall rector, and would come and stay with him at the rectory, from where they would visit many local churches.

Davy drew a ground plan of the Church (see next page) and it tells us several things, first that there was no vestry or organ room in 1831 - these both come later in the century but also of interest are the two vertical dotted lines; one is just to the west of the 'F' for font symbol; this probably marks the extent of the gallery at this date. Davy, in 1807 whilst describing the nave stated: *"At the W. end is a small gallery"*, which as we will see was moved into the tower space in the later refurbishments.

The second vertical on Davy's ground plan is just to the east of the 'P' for pulpit symbol. This could mark the position of the rood screen, Davy mentions in 1831 that: *"Part of the Screen remains"* and the antiquarian visitor in 1745 also makes a reference to the screen:*" Some Saints painted on the Screen, but obscured by the Seats".* Perhaps just the lower half of the screen remained by the 19th century.

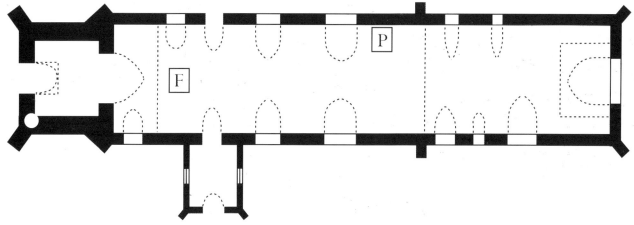

Ground plan by David Elisha Davy drawn by him on a visit to the church on December 22nd 1831.

Davy also produced outline drawings of two brasses on the chancel floor, which on his last visit in 1847 he tried to take rubbings from but with no success. His description of the chancel in 1807 is interesting: *"The Communion Table is raised one step and railed on three sides, the rails painted red. Against the south wall hangs a copperplate engraving of the Lord's Prayer, Belief and Commandments. The roof is ceiled... Over the south door is a frame of wood with an inscription about the Garthwaite charity"*.

Davy makes references during his visits in the 1840s to whitewash being removed from the font, windows' stonework and the piscina *"being recently opened"* in 1844, these operations suggest that remedial work was ongoing. However, a key restoration programme was initiated under the auspices of the rector Ellis Wade in 1863. The services of the architect J.P. St. Aubyn were employed to re-design the interior of the Church. James Piers St. Aubyn (1815-1895) was responsible for the restoration of many churches and country houses. Like many 19th century Gothic architects, such as Sir George Gilbert Scott, St. Aubyn has often been criticised for his purportedly heavy-handed restoration of many buildings, but this should be balanced by the understanding that he was a man of his times and was doing what was thought to be the right thing at the time.

The restoration work at Blaxhall included: removing the plaster ceiling and exposing the hammerbeam roof; moving the gallery from the nave into the tower; removing the remains of the rood screen which, according to George Rope, had two portraits painted in oil on wood panels, these were found when taking down one of the old 'horsebox' pews; probably the vestry was added at this date; finally, creating a new tiled floor and raising the floor in the chancel whilst re-arranging the altar area into its present layout.

Thomas Garthwaite, clerk, formerly Rector of Blaxhall, and Elizabeth his Wife, gave by their Will, a Messuage situate in Woodbridge, and known by the name of the Red Cross, and now in the occupation of John Harris; and rented at 12 pounds a year, which said sum, after necessary repairs are discharged, is to be employed, for the Clothing of poor men, women, and children, of the afore-said parish of Blaxhall, nor shall it in any wise, be a means, or occasion, to lessen, or abate, any sum or sums of money, which is, or ought to be assessed and collected, for the necessary relief of the Poor, of the said parish And as a memorial of the above, this was erected in 1762.

To provide clothing for the poor of Blaxhall, Thomas Garthwaite, in his will of 1653 left the income from the rental of the Red Cross House in Woodbridge. The board proclaiming this fact is still in the church. The charity still exists today.

The last addition of the 19th century was the organ chamber designed by Edwin Rope and added in 1897 as a Queen Victoria Diamond Jubilee memorial along with a sixth bell.

Finally, before leaving the subject of Church repairs, it might be worth mentioning some of the past reports by the archdeacon of the diocese[4], made on his regular 'visitations' to all the churches in the diocese. The old Suffolk saying of : 'what don't get done today, get done tomorrow', comes to mind when reading some of these old notes. These were 'action' lists and supposed to be completed by the archdeacon's next visit. The spelling has been transcribed as the original.

### Visitation 9th August 1676
*Mr William Aldous, rector*
*Mr Robert Warren, churchwarden*
*Mr Robert Pells, churchwarden*

*Item; The church to be whited*
*Item; The King's Arms to be newly painted and put in a frame and hanged in the Church.*
*Item; The pulpit to be close boarded*
*Item; The steeple to be sufficionally mended.*
*Item; The fence of the north side of the churchyard to be mended.*

### Visitation August 5th 1686
*Item; The Ivy about the Church and Chancel to be cutt down and destroyed.*
*Item; A new door to be made att the North Side of the Church.*

*Item; The Church to be whited*
*Item; The floar of the Church to be raised and mended.*
*Item; The leafe of the Comunion table to be mended.*
*Item; The pulpit to be lined and fringed.*
*Item: The Kings Armes to be putt into a frame and hanged upp between the Church and the Chancell.*
*Item; The ceiling of the Chancell to be lathed and also to be new tyled.*
*Item; The parsonage is in good repair accept for some little thatching which must be mended.*

### Visitation 1726
Blaxall – *The Ivy about the Church wants to be cutt down.     And the Church wants whiting.*

### Visitation 4th July 1739
*Robert Button and Thomas Bacon, churchwardens.*
*Item; The grave of Mr Zeph. Eade to be covered.*
*Item; No Commandments fixed up nor the King's Arms.*
*Item; The Register Book to be bound with an addition of parchment.*

### Visitation 3rd July 1745
*Item; A new cloath wanting for the Communion table*
*Item; The King's Arms to be fixed up.*

One wonders – was the King's coat of arms ever framed and mounted on the wall?

Work on the tower, c.1980s.

Repairs are always ongoing - this stained glass window repair and re-install was carried out by Mr Ian Free in June 2006.

# The bells

The first reference to bells in the Church is a census of 1553 when a King's Commission summoned churchwardens from each parish to supply information on their bells, plate and other assets. This census gave four bells at Blaxhall.

These particular bells must have been replaced, as a century later the next survey records five bells all dating from 1655, four of which were made by John Brend of Norwich. Remembering what problems the local parishioners had with their steeple in the 1690s, the thought does occur that these new bells might have been part of the problem! Were they too heavy or rung too much?

Davy records four of the bells being broken in 1807; however two of the bells existing today have the inscription *'John Brend, Norwich 1655'*, so possibly one wasn't as broken as Davy thought. Three of the 1655 bells were recast between 1881 and 1902. The sixth - a treble- as mentioned earlier was cast by Warners and Sons, London in 1900.

These photographs are by Ada Mannall and are some of the earliest we can date accurately. This is the 1902 bell.

The Reverend Ernest Bates and his wife Florence with the 1902 bell.

Parish Clerk Henry Shemmings and his wife Mary, with the Tenor Bell, 1902.

Alfred Bates, the young son of Ernest and Florence, who died at only six years old in 1904.

IRO K681/1/44/5

## The churchyard

There are two fine brick and Portland stone table tombs just south-east of the chancel, their inscriptions have been made indecipherable by the ravishes of centuries of Suffolk weather. In 1754 the antiquarian Thomas Martin visited the churchyard and recorded the inscription from the one table tomb that existed then, it read:

*Here lyeth*
*Nathaniel Browne*
*son of Nathl. Browne of*
*this Parish Gentleman*
*who died April the 26th 1741*
*Aged 24 years.*
*If Venture and Ingenuity could*
*have procured a long residence*
*here his Life would not have been*
*Of so short a duration but that*
*God who gave existence knew best*
*when to take it away.*

The two table tombs of the Browne family. Are these built of bricks from the local Blaxhall kiln?

The second, accompanying table tomb, would have been built five years after Martin's visit as it contains the remains of Nathaniel Browne died

5 November 1750 aged 62 and Margary Browne died April 1773 aged 78.

In medieval times churchyards were busy places; on feast days there was dancing and games, including 'fives' which was played among the buttresses of the church; fairs were held at specific times of the year and travelling merchants would set up their stalls and booths and ply a busy trade.

This is an Ada Mannall photograph of about 1905; the White Ensign flying from the tower probably indicates it was marking the 100th anniversary of the Battle of Trafalgar (see page 110). This photograph also shows the old southern boundary, with mature trees and the main gate. The area in the foreground is now part of the present churchyard.

Today the churchwarden has additional help in keeping the grass under control in the churchyard.

Blaxhall churchyard has had at least two extensions in the 20th century. One in April 1907 when there were *"alterations to the churchyard boundary by cutting down the fence between the churchyard and the covert, whereby making a gangway to the stoke-hole, and thus allowing a good deal more space for burials"*. Burials have not yet taken place in this "new space".

The second and larger addition to the churchyard was in 1932, when an area south of the then existing boundary was incorporated into the churchyard to form the present (2006) churchyard boundaries.

David Savage for many years used the old traditional method to keep the grass under control in the churchyard.

Consecration service to commemorate the extension to the churchyard, March 1932.

## Beyond the churchyard

In many parishes during the middle ages an area, frequently near the church, was set aside for community recreational pursuits; these sites were often known as 'camping closes'[5] though other names were used as well. The word 'camping' describes a game, best seen as a blend of football and handball and was played in most East Anglian counties.

The current thinking is that these sites were also used for pageants, processions and dramas, many of which involved the nearby church. The subjects of some of these medieval dramas are known, as for example, the 'Play of the Sacrament' acted out in the parish of Croxton in south-west Norfolk. The play describes how the sacred Host is systematically abused by five individuals, who then discover its redemptive powers and are converted to Christianity. The drama is played out in the open air and then, towards the end, turns into a singing procession that ends up in the sanctity of the church.

It is possible that Blaxhall had its own 'camping close' but its site is not known to us. One possible area is near the Church, as marked on the map below, where in the last few years, items of a religious association have been found.

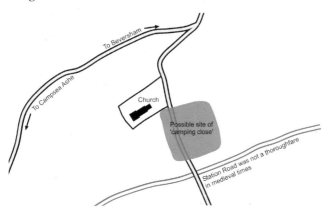

This map shows what could be a possible site for Blaxhall's 'camping close'. The brooch and key shown below were both recovered from this area.

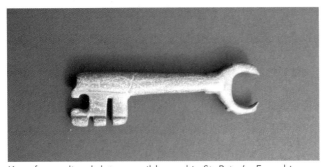

Key of a medieval date, possibly used in St. Peter's. Found in 2006 in the possible 'camping close' area.

That Blaxhall was involved in these types of festivities and customs is dramatically proven by the find of a 'Boy Bishop' token in another part of the parish in 2003. This is a unique find as the only other examples come from the large towns of Ely, Bury St. Edmunds, Ipswich and Sudbury, none are known from a small village like Blaxhall.

These tokens appear to have been issued to celebrate the reign of the children's bishop, a Christian custom known across Europe from the 13th century. The custom appears to be associated with St. Nicholas, whose feast day, December 6th, was the beginning of the Boy Bishop's reign, which lasted until Childermas or Holy Innocents (December 28th), on which day he preached a sermon and then formally resigned.

## The Boy Bishop token

During his reign the chosen boy performed, as far as that was possible, the duties of a real bishop. He wore Episcopal robes and mitre and carried a pastoral staff, and was attended by other children who acted as his chaplain, dean and other clergy. He sang Vespers and played a principal part in all church services. While his short reign lasted, he was treated with respect by everybody, feasted, entertained and given gifts.

Part of a brooch, probably worn by a priest, dating from the 14th century. The lettering on this part of the brooch makes reference to 'Jesus of Nazareth'. Found in 2003 in the possible 'camping close' area.

An Ada Mannall photograph of the church c.1907. Note the two windows seen behind the font are open at this date and letting light through.

The same view - 2007.

An Ada Mannall photograph of the font - presumably for Easter.

Blaxhall Church is decorated for all the major religious festivals during the year. A Flower Festival is often held in the summer. This display was part of the 2006 festival. The dramatic display in the font depicts 'Fire' by Florrie Shaw and Sheila Scopes.

## The Church Magazine

For over 120 years the Church magazine has been an important conveyor of church affairs and other information to the local community. The first printed magazine that included Blaxhall was produced in the 1880s and has continued, in various guises through to the present 'Ebb & Flow'.

One such edition was published (price one penny) from 1904 until 1916 and, after a hundred years, makes fascinating reading as it gives an insight into Blaxhall life in the early years of the last century. For example, we read about the Blaxhall Glee Singers (30 strong) who were entertaining the audience at Mrs Bates's Annual Concert in January 1906; that there were two Quoits Clubs in Blaxhall and a Needlework Guild. Also on the 100th Anniversary of Trafalgar Day the flag was flown from the Church and the bells rung in the evening.

Mrs Bates's Annual Concert regularly raised funds for the Church; for example, the magazine proudly announced in November 1906 that new patent burners, required to illuminate the church were to be purchased from this fund but unfortunately further enlightenment, so to speak, produced these comments in January 1907: *"..it has been found that the patent burners referred to earlier require very delicate handling and are liable to start off humming like a fog horn whenever the slightest draught is perceptible, so no change in the lighting will be made..".*

The issue of October 1914 records the winners of the Annual Rifle Club competition and that the Parish Room Library would re-open in October, H.J.S. Rope, Librarian.

Prayers were also being said for all Blaxhall men now under arms and a list was printed of who and in which unit they were serving in the Great War:

| | |
|---|---|
| Clayton Keeble | HMS Wildfire |
| Ernest Thurston | HMS Ostrich |
| Albert Ling | HMS Boadicea |
| Fred Ling | Naval Barracks, Chatham |
| Leslie Ling | Naval Barracks, Chatham |
| Charles Richardson | HMS Lawford |
| Elisha James Ling | HMS Duncan |
| Arthur James Plant | HMS Kale |
| Henry Robinson | HMS Shannon |
| Charles Richardson | Royal Garrison Artillery |
| Dan Poacher | Bedfordshire Reg. |
| James Robert Durrant | Lancashire Reg. |
| Tom Farrow | 12th Lancers |
| George Reginald Kent | Yeomanry |
| William Henry Kent | Yeomanry |
| William Airey | Kitchener's Army |
| Dick French | Kitchener's Army |
| Jack French | Kitchener's Army |
| John French | Kitchener's Army |
| Willie Friend | Kitchener's Army |
| Arthur Hammond | Kitchener's Army |
| William Hammond | Kitchener's Army |
| Fred Keeble | Kitchener's Army |
| Charles Ling | Kitchener's Army |
| James Ling | Kitchener's Army |
| Sam Ling | Kitchener's Army |
| Charles Smith | Kitchener's Army |
| Eli Smith | Kitchener's Army |
| Henry Shemmings | Kitchener's Army |
| Fred Whitehead | Kitchener's Army |
| Charles Woolnough | Kitchener's Army |

By the 1917 issues the news is generally about the war, though one highlight is the marriage of George Matthew Mannall (the son of the Stone Common shopkeeper), to Matilda Alice Ling on June 26th 1917. The news from the Front was not so good- the July issue of that year quotes: "*Charles William Richardson is suffering from trench fever and is home in England. Maurice Butcher is suffering from shell shock. Samuel Ling is wounded and is a prisoner in the hands of the Germans and Stanley Ling has been so badly wounded that he is a cripple and likely to be invalided out of the service*". The Great War was taking its toll of Blaxhall men.

"An avenue of horse-chestnut and sycamore trees has been planted along the Church path, an improvement which it is hoped the parishioners will appreciate by impressing upon the children the desirability of leaving the trees alone"
Church Magazine - December 1906

War memorial to the dead of two world wars - St. Peter's Church, Blaxhall.

The Church has been an integral part of the local community for centuries and continues to play its role in parish affairs up until the present day. For the past 100 years many church-based events have been recorded on film and a few examples are shown in the following pages.

Marriage of David and Eveline Savage. Robert and Priscilla Savage on the far left.

Wedding of 'Nipper' and Lily Ling (née Cable) c.1938.

Margaret Garnham (née Ling) with her father Abie Ling, senior.

Left to right: Mabel Farrow, Mary French and Ellen Fletcher (seated).

Marriage of Freddie Turner and Rhoda Culpeck. Rhoda ran one of the shops on Mill Common for a number of years.

A group of confirmands at Blaxhall church after the confirmation service at Snape church. Left to right: Valerie Brewster, Mollie Mayhew, Ursula Poacher, Sheila Shaw, Peter Edwards (hidden), The Reverend Browne, Roy Edwards, Margaret Reeve, Pauline Thurston, Barbara Pearce and Violet Edwards, early 1950s.

Alec Cable's wedding to Iris Richardson

Derek and Dot Keeble's wedding at Blaxhall church.

Wedding of Mary Price and Ted Smith 26 May 1951.

Ray and Sheila Scopes with their son Neil at his christening in 1965.

Wedding of Edwin and Winifred Rope 30 September 1933.

The ladies of the village waiting to see the wedding party - left to right: Mrs Smith (Policeman Smith's wife), Linda Olding holding Mabel Olding's skirt, Muriel Olden with daughters Carol and Susan (clinging to her mother's legs), Ivy Davidson, Marjorie Cady, Marian Davidson (née Brewster), Mrs Alice Woolnough with her daughter Gillian, Violet Richardson, Elizabeth Drewery, Mrs Alice Denny (née Hammond).

Wedding of John Leeks and Shirley Taylor, 2005. The Reverend Barrie Slater is in charge of the camera as well as being the minister in charge of the service!

Funeral of Derek Keeble, November 1996, The Reverend Margaret Blackall presided over the service.

Blaxhall Church choir, c.1957. Back row left to right: Fred Emsden, Carol Coggins, Paul Smith, Ruth Fayers, Laurie Ling, Christine Ling, Barry Messenger and Marian Burch. Second row from back: Sheila Scopes, Violet Skeet, Frank Shaw, Rosemary Browne, Molly Pictor and Arthur Smith. Third row: Cynthia Jay, Mabel Farrow, Mary French, Ellen Fletcher, Reverend Browne, Mrs Browne, Florrie Shaw and Shirley Leeks. Front row: Beverely Dunn, Angela Jay, Robert Burch and Susan Coggins.

# CHAPTER SIX
# THE SCHOOL'S STORY

## Part 1 - Rise and Fall

Although it is evident that some schooling was available for the village's children well before the 19th century, notably in the old School House on Mill Common, it was not until 1851 that a purpose built school was opened for all the children of the village's poor and less well off. At that time such voluntary schools were being built at private expense all over the country under the auspices of the National Society (an offshoot of the SPCK); thus Blaxhall was a National or church school. The building was financed and built on land owned by John George Sheppard, one of Blaxhall's squires and a substantial landowner in the area.

When Blaxhall National School opened in 1851, it consisted of one large classroom, (length 44' 8", breadth 17' 6", height 11' 10"), lighted by several windows, including a large one at the end of the building facing the road; joined on to the school was a small cottage for the head teacher; these two buildings can be identified on the south of the present Youth Hostel. There was a movable partition in the long high classroom and a gallery at one end; the gallery was a series of tiered platforms reaching almost to ceiling height on which the "scholars" (as they were called) could with difficulty be seated. Although this took up a sizeable area of precious floor space, it had the great advantage that one person, usually the headteacher or the Rector, could instruct the whole school, thus freeing up a member of staff for other work. But there was a disadvantage: *"22 Feb 1872 A lesson omitted in consequence of time devoted to marching on and off the gallery"* states an entry in the school log book. Outside was a playground of about 1,000 square yards with turf and pine trees, probably enclosed by a white paling fence; boys' and girls' earth closets were at the rear of the building and

some tin wash basins with water being carried from the well near today's bottle bank; the school bell hung at the western end of the building.

In the 1860s the number on the school roll was usually about 90, but the average weekly attendance was well below this figure for a variety of reasons: in the first place, attendance was not compulsory (it became so in 1876 for all five to 13 year olds); then, there were epidemics of measles, whooping cough, diphtheria and the usual children's ailments; severe weather conditions would keep the children away, particularly the "distance children" as those who lived in the far flung regions were called; and of course there were the constant requirements from the farmers for children, often as young as six or seven, to work in the fields picking up stones, scaring crows, singling beet, topping clover, picking peas or potatoes, as well as older boys being given leave for 'brushing' and 'blocking' for local shooting parties. The school took in children of all ages up to 12 or more (including babies as young as 14 months whose mothers needed to go out to work), but many children left school much earlier, the girls to go into service, the boys to permanent fieldwork – this being necessary to supplement their farm worker fathers' often meagre wages. To teach the large number of scholars there were only a headteacher and an assistant; one or two monitors, usually girls who had just left school, were employed to help with the babies and to perform menial tasks around the school – sweeping the floors, keeping the fires in, emptying buckets and so on.

So that was the picture in the school's early years: 60 or 70 children in regular attendance, a headteacher and assistant, with the Rector teaching Scripture or

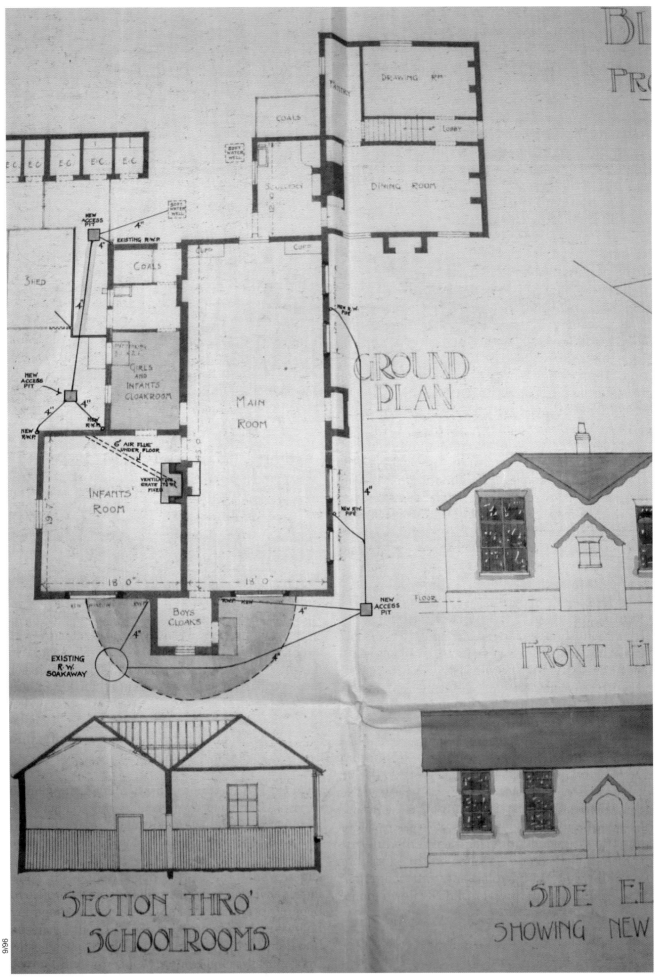

9/96

Part of 1923 site plan for new windows and other repairs to the school.

Blaxhall School after it's conversion to a Youth Hostel. The school's well, foreground.

at least visiting on an almost daily basis. But with the continuing rise in population and with school attendance being made compulsory, urgent steps had to be taken to accommodate the increased numbers. So, in 1879 a new classroom was built on the northeast end of the school about half the length but the same breadth and height as the first classroom:

### 1879

*"November 9: The newly built classroom was used for the first time, Standard I in charge of the assistant removed there. This has given more desk room to the upper Standards and the order of the whole school has been better in consequence".*

This was to remain the school's basic classroom accommodation until its closure 83 years later. However, continual improvements, but not extensions, were made in the intervening years in efforts to accommodate the increasing number of children which rose to a peak of 143 on the roll by 1894.

### 1889

*"Great alterations in the school premises. It is now warm, light and commodious."*

### 1891

*"The Managers have decided to reopen the school as a free school; they agree to accept the grant of 10 shillings per head in lieu of school fees."*

### 1893

*Report of H.M. Inspector "Main room: blocking south door, more light from the east; pan system or more frequent emptying for the foul offices; urinal for boys. Infants' room; enlarge west window; and remove antiquated gallery......"*

### 1902

*End of Voluntary Management. The school will reopen under the County Council Authority (Educational).* i.e. maintained but not provided by the local authority.

### 1910

*HMI report: "Main room is divided by movable partition....... If glazed and put into working order it would be a great boon to the organisation. The warming by a small tortoise stove is inadequate".*

And so it went on until in 1922 notice was received that as from the 1st January the school was to

_Friday 2nd Attendances 69 & 71 Average for the week 7.01_

_Monday 5th Morning attendance 40 Afternoon 69 rather small on account of the pea-harvest, several children being employed in picking up peas._

_Tuesday 6th Numbers low on account of a rainy day. Morning attendance 59 Afternoon 47_

_The Rector paid a short visit to the school._

_Wednesday 7th Morning attendance 82 Afternoon a holiday – Children's school treat._

_Thursday 8th Morning attendance 77 Afternoon 73_

Excerpt from an early (1867) school logbook entry.

become a Council school, i.e. maintained and provided (rented in our case) by the local authority, and in 1949 the property was put up for sale with the rest of the Ullswater estate. It was not until the 1950s that electric lighting, taps with running water and efficient heating were installed but flushing toilets never appeared whilst the school was in use, the Inspector's report for 1959 noting that "Elsan toilets have replaced the buckets"; in 1961 a telephone was installed "Snape 391". Blaxhall school had at last caught up with the 20th century (except for the loos!) but within the year came the not unexpected news from the Ministry of Education that it was to be closed at the end of the summer term. From its peak of 143 in 1894, numbers on the school roll had steadily declined (1914, ninety-three; 1925, seventy-eight; 1937, sixty-one; 1941, forty-one; 1953, 31; 1957, twenty-five) so that its closure had become inevitable: _"27th July 1962 Blaxhall Church Primary school closed today.... There are eighteen children on the roll ages five – 11 plus. 17 of these are being transferred to Snape C.P School and one girl will be transferred to Butley S.M. school"._

However, the premises were not to remain empty for long: The Youth Hostel Association bought the building and in early 1965 opened it as the only Youth Hostel in Suffolk, replacing the one closed at Felixstowe in 1959. In early days it slept only 25 and people had to do their own cooking, but today, whilst still the only Youth Hostel in Suffolk, it has been greatly extended and modernised so that it sleeps up to 50 and there are excellent kitchen, dining and studying facilities. People of all ages, often in parties, stay there literally from all over the world and throughout the year; it is more often

than not fully booked at weekends from March to October, during holidays and many weekends during the winter months.

During the Second World War, schoolchildren from London's East End were evacuated to Blaxhall in September 1939 and again in July 1944 (see page 130); nowadays, ten or twelve times a year, primary school parties from London's East end stay at the hostel. Under the auspices of the Country Trust, a locally based charity, they visit a number of local attractions – Minsmere for pond dipping, Orford castle, a working farm and so on – but one of the highlights of their visits is the night walks on the common; their excitement is intense when, often for the first time, they experience real darkness, see the stars and planets, hear the sound of silence interrupted perhaps by a screech owl or a strange deer bark, see a glow-worm or a bat. So its old walls still echo the buzz of schoolchildren's voices almost 160 years on.

Readers who wish to learn more about village school life generally are referred to Flora Thompson's charming evocation of it in the late 19th century in her trilogy "Lark Rise to Candleford", chapters 11 & 12, and for school life in the early 1950s to Miss Read's "Village School", a delightful picture where primitive drains coexist with an efficient school meals service. For Blaxhall school in particular, see George Ewart Evans's _"Ask the Fellows who Cut the Hay"_, chapter 20, and the school log books 1866 – 1962 held in the Suffolk Records Office Ipswich, which provide some fascinating insights; extracts from these log books looking at a couple of aspects of schooldays form the next section of this chapter.

# Part 2. CHILDREN! CHILDREN! and some Special Days
## Extracts from the log books 1866-1920

### 1866

**Oct 9:** *Dismissed School at half past eleven o'clock, the school being lent to the Steward to take Rents.*
**Oct 18:** *No School. A Club being served in the schoolroom for children's clothing.*
**Oct 31:** *Boys out 'brushing' for Mr Garrett at Glemham - gave 45 leave.*
**Nov 14:** *Boys had leave for 'blocking' for Mr Garrett.*

### 1867

**Jan 30:** *Two monitors scolded severely for breaking up thoughtlessly some picture boards but forgiven on evincing penitence.*
**Feb 20:** *Children required at home while their mothers were in the fields.*
**Feb 28:** *The elder children employed in scaring crows and picking up stones.*

### 1868

**Jan 27:** *The Rector visited the school and dismissed John Wardley for rushing out of the school when about to be corrected for bad behaviour.*
**Feb 26:** *Ash Wednesday. Children went to church in the morning, had half holiday in the afternoon.*
**Mar 24:** *Admitted Andrew Livett, age 10 years, to the third standard,*
**Mar 25:** *The boy Andrew Livett bears a very bad character and as he had spoken impertinently to the Mistress and injured a little boy by throwing a stone, he was sent away at noon and his name erased from the books.*
**Jul 13:** *Several children gone into the fields singling beet.*
**Aug 5:** *Attendance rather small, several children being employed in picking peas.*
**Sep 28:** *Morning attendance only 55…..eleven children ill, two dead.*
**Sep 30:** *Thirteen children ill and many kept away because of the infection.*

### 1869

**Apr 13:** *Admitted Mollie Keeble age 1 year, 7 months to the babies' class.*
**Sep 16:** *Several children gleaning.*

BELOW: Left back row: Ray Hewitt, Douglas Smith, 'Ginger', John Ling, Ray Poacher, Ernie Ling, Lottie Ling, Charles Ling, Margaret Ling. Front row: Percy Drewery, Arthur Drewery and Gladys Ling.

Harvest time was a time when everyone had a job to do.. even the children. Here they have stopped to be photographed whilst pursuing rabbits.

## 1870

*Apr 4:* Admitted Florence Ling age 1 year, 2 months; Sarah Ling age 1 year 8 months and Mollie Plant age 3 yrs, 3 months.
*Jul 15:* Set a class of elder girls to industrial work in the mistress' house.

## 1871

*Feb 6:* Two girls crossed from the register, gone to service.
*Mar 13:* E. Ling and Lucy Gooding engaged as monitoresses for the Infants.
*Jun 12:* Readmitted Robert and Mary Jay, both to the Infants as the latter, although 12 years of age, is innocent of the Alphabet.
*Dec 21:* Half holiday to enable children to get their Christmas gift of beef.

## 1872

*Jan 13:* Two girls severely punished for wilfully burning one of the younger children with a red hot poker.
*Feb 27:* Several complaints from the children, especially dinners stolen.
*Feb 29:* Endeavoured to show the children the great sin of petty dishonesty and to encourage the thief to confess his or her fault privately.
*Mar 4:* Discontinued Lucy Gooding's name on the register. No complaints of losses since.
*Nov 24:* The children marched in the playground during marching time.

## 1873

*Jan 9:* Children rather unsteady on account of the Treat.
*Jan 10:* No school. Mrs Sheppard's annual Xmas Treat.
*Jul 22:* Babies allowed ¾ of an hour in the playground. Very hot!
*Sep 24:* Babies marched and were taught in the playground.
*Oct 24:* Gallery Scripture lesson. Pupil teacher given time for mapping.

## 1879

*Feb 28:* In the afternoon the policeman came in to warn the boys about throwing stones at the bell and the building. Took the names of the principal offenders, Thomas and William Thurston, Henry Keeble, Albert Poacher and T. Woolnough.

## 1880

*Oct 14:* Reproved Miriam Ling and Maria Poacher for using bad language in the Playground, also some of the boys for fighting.

## 1881

*Oct 11:* Several children staying away because of bad boots, the roads being very dirty.

## 1883

*Feb 20:* Four boys removed for insulting two transfers by spitting upon them.
*Mar 16:* John Ling detained after school for one and half hours for knocking John Airey's teeth out.
*Apr 24:* Four boys detained after school for ill-using two little girls on their way home at noon.

## 1894

*Nov 8:* The parents of Oscar Ling have taken him away from school age 11 years 9 months. The mother informed the Attendance Committee that unless they granted leave to go to work, she would have to go into the Workhouse.

## 1895

*June 28:* Children promised an outing to Aldboro' as an inducement to regular attendance.
*Aug 2:* Children to Aldeburgh. Waggons were provided by the farmers and friends also. In spite of threatening morning, a most enjoyable day's outing was given to 130 children.

## 1896

*May 6:* Wrote to F Ling Esq. asking him not to allow children to pick stones on his land when ought to be at school.
*Sep 4:* School visited by the Hon. William Lowther* who saw the children drill and heard them sing.(*Father of J W Lowther, 1st Viscount Ullswater, 1855 to 1948, Speaker of the House of Commons 1905 to 1921).
*Sep 16:* Holiday given on account of Campsea Ashe flower show.

## 1897

*June 21:* School closed for Tuesday and Wednesday on account of the Queen's Diamond Jubilee.
*Sep 13:* Five of Barnado's children taken away en route to Canada.
*Nov 5:* The result of proceedings taken against

Blaxhall School c. 1907.

Infants of 1907 with (probably) Mrs Whitehead.

*several parents for irregular attendance has improved attendance considerably.*

## 1898

*Apr 25: Lizzie Ling appointed to take care of the babies.*
*Jul 8: Holiday given to allow the teachers and some of the children to attend the East Suffolk Sewing Scheme Exhibition. Our successes were: 1 first prize, 2 second prizes and 26 first class certificates.*
*Sep 26: Admitted six children from Dr Barnado's.*

## 1899

*May 8: An outbreak of diptheria has caused panic amongst the parents...*

## 1900

*Jan 26: Influenza, whooping cough, colds and children's ailments generally have reduced the average to 76. No on books 121.*
*May 24: Ascension Day children taken to church. Holiday in afternoon in honour of the Relief of Mafeking. (The fortress city in South Africa, commanded by Col. Baden-Powell, had been besieged by the Boer forces for seven months).*

## 1901

*Jul 12: Attendance fell on Friday on account children absent to attend the Earl of Guilford's home coming (wedding).*

## 1902

*Jun 20: School closed for one week on account of the King's Coronation.*

## 1905

*Nov 22: Albert Ling was punished for disorderly conduct. I gave him several strokes on his hinder parts with the stick.*

## 1907

*May 31: Empire Day celebrated. In the morning lessons were given on "The Flag" and "Our Empire". Patriotic songs were sung. A procession formed by the children marched round the village; halts were made at various points, songs were sung and the flag saluted. In the afternoon sports were provided for the children in a meadow. At 4:30 the children sat down to a bountiful tea provided by Mr & Mrs John Wardley of Red House Farm.*

## 1911

*Jun 16: School closed for Coronation, 1 week.*
*Nov 12: Nine boys absent to attend Lord Rendlesham's funeral at Campsea Ashe.*

## 1912

*Jun 12: Sent cricket team to Snape. Blaxhall won by 6 wickets.*
*Jun 20: Mr Creak, gardening instructor visited. Boys marked out plots and commenced work.*

## 1914

*Oct: Drill Report... I should also advise that boys be allowed to remove collars and coats during exercise and that the wearing of large and unsuitable hats by the girls be discouraged*

## 1915

*Feb 15: Children gave a concert in the Parish Room for the benefit of the sick and wounded in the war.*
*May 13: School closed by medical authority in consquence of outbreak of Scarlet Fever.*

This is an Ada Mannall photograph of c. 1910, recording the harvesting of the annual blackberry crop.

## 1917

*Sep 20: Holiday to collect blackberries. About 24 st. was collected and over £2 was paid for them.*

## 1919

*Aug 8: School closes for Harvest Holidays for six weeks. The extra week is given by the King's wish to mark the conclusion of the Great War and the signing of peace.*

Year of c. 1900

Year of 1925/6 - Head Teacher is Mrs Ollis - Florrie Shaw is seated girl third from the left.

Blaxhall School c.1939.

Blaxhall Schoolchildren, 1949 - Mrs Florence Evans (left) and Miss Packard (right).

# Part 2 - Within Living Memory

Today's two oldest true Blaxhallites (that is born and lived all their lives in the village) benefited from that extra week's holiday in 1919: Florrie Shaw (née Ling) and Peter Fletcher were both born just before the First World War and started school in 1919, *"28th April, School reopened. Bitterly cold. Admitted 4 children"* is the bald entry in the log book, but for Florrie and Peter it was a big day. Peter recalls walking reluctantly from his home on Mill Common, where he still lives, across the track and over the common to the school a few stones' throw away, which reminds him that a year or two later he was punished by the headmaster for throwing stones from the playground onto the roof of the Smithy across the road. Specific dates and events fade as time goes by, although, as all small boys would, he remembers at the age of three in 1917 being taken by his father to see the Zeppelin at Theberton which had passed in flames over Blaxhall before it crashed.

Florrie had a longer walk to school. She lived on Stone Common with her six brothers and two sisters and the twice daily return journeys they made in all weathers are still clear in her memory – twice daily because they returned home for their dinners out of school at 12 o'clock, scurry home for a quick meal and back again by 1 o'clock and then a more leisurely walk home after school at three or four o'clock; no wonder a shoemaker had set up shop on Stone Common generations earlier. Florrie has many other memories which include the school parties going blackberry picking each year, the games on the heath, walks to Iken Cliff and of sewing and needlework which she still enjoys.

The headmaster during Florrie's and Peter's first few years was Frederick James 'Billy' Whitehead, a notable figure in the school's story. He was appointed in October 1888 and retired in July 1922, his headship spanning almost a third of the school's 111 years, and covering the momentous times at the end of Queen Victoria's reign and the cataclysm of the First World War in which so many of his former pupils gave their lives; his wife, and later on his daughter Evelyn, were assistant teachers at his side for many of those years; sadly Evelyn died in 1913 at the age of 25. His Majesty's Inspector's report of November 1921 reads: *"It is more than 30 years since the Headmaster took charge of the school. He has grown to be part of the village life, and his good influence has reached every home, parent and child. His*

*service to the school will come to an end in the near future and it is due to him to place on record his faithful and careful work....his impress upon his scholars may be traced wherever they go.....*" On retirement he and his wife went to live in Woodbridge, but less than 18 months later he died at the age of 67 and was brought back to the village to which he had given such devoted service and lies buried with his daughter in St Peter's churchyard.

Billy Whitehead (far right) was headmaster of Blaxhall school for over 34 years.

The School Managers during most of Florrie's and Peter's time were Mrs Cholmeley, (née Darling) Miss Edith Rope, Mr Edwin Rope, Mr Thomas Gaze, Revd. T.C. Wilson and Mr R.H.S. Sherwood (Correspondent i.e. secretary). Mrs Cholmeley, the daughter of the Rector of Eyke, came to Blaxhall shortly before the First World War and was to suffer the sadness of her only son being killed at Ypres in 1915. She lived in the cottage next door to Peter, the former miller's house, and remained a School Manager/ Correspondent until shortly before her death in 1948 at the age of 87.

Florrie left school in 1928 (school leaving age had been raised after the war to 14, or 15 if you had no job to go to) and went to work for the Mannalls (see page 57) on Stone Common as nursemaid to their two children; four years later she took up a position as maid to Lady Blanche Cobbold at Glemham Hall.

Peter was moved by his parents, shortly after headmaster Whitehead's retirement, to the school in Tunstall where he remained until 1929 when he started his first job at Leiston Works making steam engines and buses. At about the same time as Florrie and Peter left school, Ray Poacher was born at High Terrace; he also remembers his first day at school in 1933 when he was sat upon the rocking horse to settle him down a bit and, like Florrie, recalls the daily treks from Mount Pleasant to and from school in all weathers. The rocking horse, incidentally, had been bought in 1917 *"for £3.10s off Clara F. Toller, the Estate Office, Blaxhall."* Ray and his friend Henry Hammond have many other memories of their days at the school: "Breathing exercises every morn then singing hymns before lessons" "Derek Keeble and myself getting the cane for throwing stones" "gardening lessons in the afternoons, every boy with his own plot and rewards for best turn out and best veggies, the girls did not have a garden plot they stayed in doing needlework, the eldest girls tidied the teacher's house" "rehearsing plays at Grove Farm put on by Mrs Edwin Rope" "swimming lessons in the summer at Langham bridge" and so on. Ray left Blaxhall school just before the outbreak of the Second World War in 1939 to go to Wickham Market school (secondary schools had by then been set up). He and the other children were supplied at Local Education Authority expense with "new bicycles, waterproof capes and leggings for the journey".

In the year that Ray left Blaxhall school, young Henry Hammond from Old Barn Cottages started, his elder sister Ena was already there and his younger sister, Daphne, would join them before the end of the war with her best friend Daphne Savage. Henry was at the school during the whole of the war 1939-1945; he recalls that after being there a few months he was still not very good at counting and his teacher, Miss Whiting, would "run him round the table making him count the legs "one, two, three, four" and soon tap him on the knuckles if he faltered"; he has many other memories shared with Ray's.

Terry Skeet was a fellow pupil at this time and both Henry and Terry remember the evacuees from the East End of London coming to the village just after the start of the war, two boys aged 10 or 11 to Henry's and his sisters' household, which with only two bedrooms made for rather a squeeze, and two girls, Dawn and Doris, to the Skeet's at Lime Tree Cottage. Terry recalls he and his brother Ivan feeling it "very strange having two girls in our house suddenly and very difficult on Friday bath night with hot water from the copper into a bungalow bath and a blanket on a line separating us…….We all walked to school together; if there was an air raid siren we went home together but only in twos and we were taught to lie on the ground if a plane came." Interestingly, the forty or so evacuees from West Ham, accompanied by two

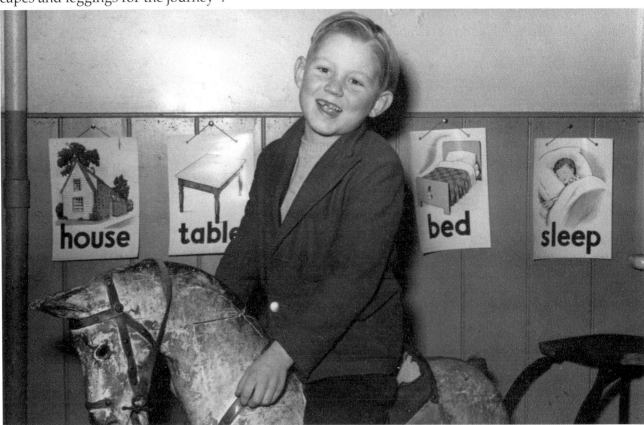

George Poacher on the rocking horse c. 1950s.

Both these photographs are of the school Open day in July, 1949, even though there is a May Queen (see page 130).

teachers, arrived in Blaxhall within three weeks of the declaration of war on 3rd September 1939 , the school log book recording: *Sep 18: "School reopened for all children….. Too many for space. Sep 25: School sessions: Blaxhall children a.m. Evacuees p.m.Oct 2: A few evacuees removed to other districts".*

They remained in Blaxhall for the next eight months, when within a week of the start of the Dunkirk evacuation, 24th May 1940, and the great threat of invasion, possibly on the East coast: *May 27: "Received notice the London children to be moved to safer area. Jun 1: School reopened this Saturday morning for evacuees to assemble and bring any parcels to be forwarded to new addresses".* (Brinklow, near Coventry!).

Less than three weeks later on 17th June, 120 German bombers attacked eastern England by night, the raid which marked the start of what came to be called the Blitz. But that was not the end of the evacuees in Blaxhall: four years later in mid June 1944, the flying bomb V-1 raids started on London and by 6th July 10,000 houses had been destroyed and 2,752 people killed, a far higher casualty rate than during the Blitz: *Jul 22: "Receiving this morning, Saturday, a notification from LEA that evacuees should be admitted on Monday, I went to each house concerned and delivered the message. Jul 24: 12 evacuees admitted into the school".*

Blaxhall's links with children from the East End continue to this day, as we saw at the beginning of this chapter. During 1944, the County Library agreed to open a juvenile section in the school, this remained until its closure, and on November 23rd the school was visited by a Colonel of the American Airforce stationed at Parham. February 1945 saw the introduction of a school meals service (not free to all) provided from kitchens in Tunstall but on March 6th *"Mr Palmer arrived at 12.25 to say the oven would not heat, so he bought two tins of luncheon meat.."* - after all it was still wartime!

By the end of the war Daphne Savage, Daphne Hammond, Violet Edwards, Sheila Shaw, Mollie Mayhew, shortly to be followed by Shirley Hewitt and others were at the school whose numbers had now declined to about 40. Mrs Watmough, a rather authoritarian figure, was headteacher in 1947/1948: *"The Head Teacher has forbidden the kicking of balls in the playground" "Dawn French sent home at noon as she is not eligible for free dinners" "All children told not to come to school too early but to wait for the whistle".*

Daily milk for all schoolchildren was the government order of the day, so in Blaxhall Fred Mayhew, the local milkman, "used to bring the milk in two large cans and hand it out in jugs, the children had their own beakers, some had jam jars; later it was delivered in third of a pint bottles". They all remember the Open Day in July 1949 when Mrs Evans, the headmistress since September 1948, organised *"singing, acting, flute playing, Maypole dancing, boxing. A good attendance of parents.*
*£3-3s-6d collected through sales of refreshments etc. This will be used for a school Christmas party".* According to Terry Skeet "Mr Evans taught us to box using real boxing gloves, holding a large pad up for us to hit"; Mr Evans also used to act as a supply teacher when the staff were short-handed and of course most of his famous book was written within the four walls of the school house.

His wife, Florence Evans, was to remain headmistress until 1956 with her assistant teacher Miss Packard. The school, although steadily decreasing in numbers, was a happy and enlightened place to be as all her former pupils recall. HMI's report for March 1953 states: *"The Headmistress has charge of 19 juniors and her assistant 12 infants…..both are indefatigable workers, wholly devoted to the well-being of the children; both exert a cultured and refining influence…..they are to be congratulated on the wholesome atmosphere that characterises the school".*

Indeed, in those years the school does seem to have been transformed into one not only where academic levels were being greatly improved (Mrs Evans had a BA Hons from London University and postgraduate training at Cambridge) but where other cultural and physical activities were being nurtured: concerts and dancing sessions with other schools often in the parish room; music was being taught both in the school and outside,

Miss Packard gives a nature study class.

132

On Tuesday, 11th May, 1954 we all set out to explore Church Pit.
Here we are at the entrance to the pit.

Natural history lessons were sometimes held in the pit by the village hall and were a favourite lesson when Florence Evans was headmistress.

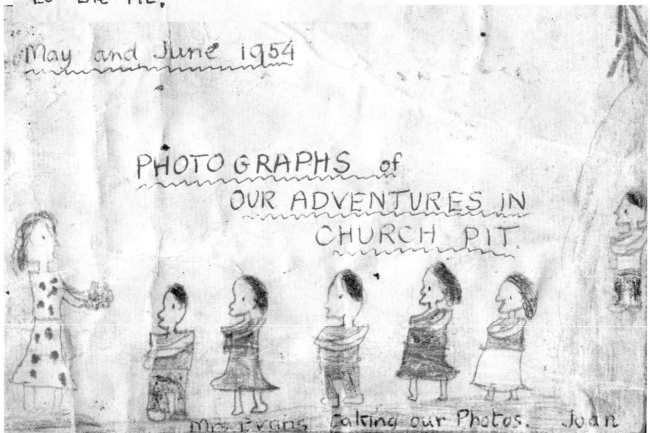

May and June 1954

PHOTOGRAPHS of
OUR ADVENTURES IN
CHURCH PIT.

Mrs Evans taking our Photos.     Joan

Local people participated in the local history event organised by George Ewart Evans in April, 1951. This photograph shows two of them - Henry Keeble (left) and Robert Savage.

notably the piano by Mrs Ellen Fletcher; inter schools games tournaments being held – Blaxhall were ace at mixed touch rugby, four boys, four girls; PT, boxing, and swimming with tests for 25 yards, 50 yards, even 100 yards at Langham bridge; school harvest festivals with vegetable and fruit being carried up to the church, and jumble sales in aid of school funds; whole school outings to Ipswich to see the Coronation film and visit Christchurch Mansion, picnicking in the park and so on and on. There are particular memories also of the Local History Exhibition in 1951, with 150 children from neighbouring schools visiting; also of "gathering acorns to sell to the Forestry, one and a half tons were collected and £44.10.9 were paid out", a lot of this going into the children's pockets, often to help them pay for school meals, as the late Bert Smith recalled; and, not least, of the coming of Infantile Paralysis to some of their classmates and of measles epidemics *"only 11 out of 36 children present"*; of dentists, doctors, and of the regular inspections by a rather fierce nurse for "nits", which some villagers are still half convinced to this day were first brought to Blaxhall by the war-time evacuees - "pull them like peas you could" "lousy as cuckoos they were".

*A short digression here on Florence and George Ewart Evans, whose influence and impact on the village is still felt half a century later.*

The **Evans family**, including four children under the age of nine, came to Blaxhall in 1948 when Florence took over the headship of the village school. For her interview for the job, Florence had walked the three miles from Campsey Ash station and back again after travelling from London by train. The family had fallen on difficult times during and after the war: their home at Sawston near Cambridge, where Florence and George had met whilst teaching at the same school before the war, had burnt down and whilst George was away serving in the RAF, Florence had taken her two children to live with her mother in a small semi-detached in Enfield. There was great concern as to what should happen to them all when George finally left the RAF – he disliked teaching, he wanted to be a writer and his increasing deafness meant he felt the number of career options open to him were now reduced.

So, the family's move in 1948 from surburban London to what seemed to be "the middle of nowhere" was quite a risk and also came as quite shock – from 'all mod. cons.' suburbia to a remote village with no electricity, no sanitation, no running water, the nearest telephone a mile away and only a twice weekly bus service to civilisation at Saxmundham. The idea was that, in a rather unusual reversal, for the time, of conventional roles, Florence would teach and be the family's main breadwinner while George, looking after the

George Ewart Evans in the school house garden with (left to right) Matthew, Mary, Susan and Jane.

younger children, would write poetry and stories and occasional radio scripts for the BBC. People in Blaxhall realised how difficult life was for the family in the early years; Mrs Reeve, the school housekeeper, gave them cooked food saying "it was for the children", as she saw a family close to the breadline. Another time at Christmas a plucked chicken ready for the oven was left on the school doorstep.

In 1952, George's deafness caused him to acquire a hearing aid and in the same year a recording machine was lent to him by the BBC; these were to transform his life, and eventually his family's fortunes. Sitting in the schoolhouse trying to write poetry and fiction, it slowly began to dawn on him that under his very nose was the subject that was going to occupy him for the rest of his life. He realised that he was living in a village populated by farm workers who had lived through the virtual disappearance of the horse as the main presence on the farm, and into a period of increasing mechanisation. He realised that it would be an important piece of social history to record the voices, experiences, attitudes, the feelings of these people before they died and their memories were lost forever. From his research came, what must be classed as a seminal work – *Ask the Fellows who Cut the Hay*"(Faber & Faber, 1956) and then a

further ten related books over the next 30 years.

In the year that "Ask the Fellows.." was published the family left Blaxhall, Florence having secured a job as head of a much larger school in Needham Market. Although they had lived in the village for only eight years, Florence left a lasting influence for good on a generation of village children

In September 1958, Mrs Ella Salt succeeded as headmistress of the 28 children at the school, with Miss Alice Packard still in charge of the infants group. Poor Mrs Salt!, in her four years at the school until March 1961 she seemed to have one problem after another (not including the children) to deal with:

*1958 Jan. 17*: *"This morning it was not possible to bring the children into school, due to thick smoke and bad fumes. They were taken for a nature walk on the heath. All doors and windows had to be left open to clear the smoke which took about an hour and a half. Windows were open all day".*

*Apr. 19:* *"Two new heating stoves delivered to the school".*

But the problem was not yet sorted, a year later:

A school photograph of Poppy Smith (née Hewitt),
1933 aged ten.

A school photograph of Ronnie Keeble, 1933.

**1959 Jan. 27:** *"There is a prevalence of dry throats and persistent coughing among the children. Coke fumes suspected of causing same."*
**Jan 28, 29, 30:** *"Children complain of headaches and feeling sickly".*

**Mar. 16:** *"Main classroom out of use owing to smoke rising from the floorboards".*

*6.45pm Fire Service was called in to inspect intensely hot chimney- fire grate removed in north classroom- soot and debris smouldering behind grate- an outbreak of fire possible at any time. Firemen left at 9.20pm".*

Then the boiler began to leak and the cesspits overflowed and the ailing Miss Packard was absent yet again, when she came back after a prolonged absence "the children subscribed and presented Miss Packard with a parting gift of a cushion and cover". But only a few months later Miss Packard died. Then in April 1959 " *Head Teacher absent part*

*days each week with official sanction during Mr Salt's grave illness"*, from which it appears he died later that year. No wonder Ella Salt after all those trials and tribulations, succumbed to illness herself and by March 1961 she was absent through illness and left the school at the end of that month.

When the school opened after the Easter holiday, Margery E Burton (permanent supply staff) took charge; numbers were steadily declining with 23 on the role. Mrs Burton presided over the last 15 months of the school's existence seemingly without the ill luck that Ella Salt had had, although there was still occasional trouble with fumes from the stove and doubts arose about the quality of the drinking water. There were endless visits from officials during this period: 'Schools Welfare Officer', 'Clerk of Works', 'Official Groundsmen', 'PE Organiser', 'School Meals Organiser', 'Chief Education Officer', Educational Physiologist'. The School Managers held a meeting (in the event it turned out to be their last one), in July 1961, those present being Rev. E S Browne (chairman), Mr Alden (correspondent), Mrs Savage, Mr F Reeve, at which the drinking water was declared "free from contamination, therefore water would not now be required from Tunstall School". After the mid-summer holiday the school became a one teacher establishment with 19 on the role. Mrs Lilian Newby the former school head until 1944, was taken on as clerical assistant for six hours per week.

Then came the first public indication of official interest in the future viability of the school when in November two representatives from the County Treasurer's Department visited and on March 6 1962 *"an official Ministry of Education notice to close Blaxhall School received from the Correspondent and fixed in a prominent position by the main door".* The following week outbreaks of Scarlet Fever and German Measles occurred amongst the children. The school's final term started with 18 on the role and on June 26 notice was received that *"Blaxhall CP School is to be closed at the end of the current term… arrangements are being made by the East Suffolk Education Authority to transport all Blaxhall children to Snape School from the beginning of next term".* In early July the Headmaster of Snape School visited and spoke to the children about their transfer in September; this was followed by a visit to Snape School by all 18 children with their parents.

On July 27 1962 Margery Burton signed off in the logbook and recorded that:

**58**

*1962*

The following facts concerning Blaxhall School may be of interest to record: —

Mrs. M.E. Reeve (née Jay), the school caretaker, who has served in this capacity for almost 21 years, is the grand-daughter of Celia Poacher, who entered the school as a pupil in March 1865, aged 4 years 7 months, and is No. 3 on the original Admission Register.

re The last child admitted here — on January 10th. 1962 — Alan Keith Church is the great-great nephew of Elvina Ling, who was the first child admitted — March 1864. // (she is No. 4 on the original Admission Register, because the entries were apparently made in alphabetical order of Christian name.)

M.E.B.

Last entry in the school logbook.

Blaxhall schoolgirls in fancy dress, c.1950s. Left to right June Chandler (née Keeble ), Mollie Pictor (née Mayhew), Elsie Willis (née Thurston), Sheila Scopes (née Shaw), Daphne Renfro (née Hammond),  Gloria Sage (née Messenger ), Blanche Knights (née Curtis), Pauline Pierce (née Thurston), Margaret Churchyard (née Reeve), Eileen ? (née Keeble).

Blaxhall School Rugby Touch Team, 1951.

# CHAPTER SEVEN
# AND FINALLY - FOLKS!

We had no end of discussion and changes of mind (and sleepless nights) in deciding on the fittest way to end this medley of a book of Blaxhall people, places and pictures! Should it comprise of a further mix along the same lines? Should there be separate sections on 'women of Blaxhall' and 'men of Blaxhall'? If so, who should be included and who might be upset at those not included? Should a section be devoted to the late Chris Long's super set of portraits of some present day Blaxhall folk, first displayed at our Blaxhall's Living Past exhibition in 2005? Or should we once again, as Chris had done, send a note to every Blaxhall household inviting the occupants to be photographed for our archives and for this book? Should we not have this final chapter at all? Who might be unintentionally offended by what we did and did not include? – and so on and so forth.

In the end, we decided simply to take a final dip into our extensive photographic archive, which

after all is where the idea for this book began, and to finish with a 'portrait gallery of Blaxhall folk' from our earliest snapshot, c.1850, up to the end of the last century. Most of the images are of individuals, couples or families but we also have in our archives a number of fascinating group photographs, such as the ones appearing earlier in this book and the ones shown below. We have then added to the final pages the photographs that Chris Long took for BAG in 2005.

For those who are interested, our photographic archives can be accessed on the Blaxhall Archive data base and at the Suffolk Records Office – they are well worth visiting.

This is not the end of the work of the Blaxhall Archive Group - it is still open for business - we are only too happy to accept photographs, postcards, documents that we can copy and incorporate in the archives.

Off to the river on a hot summer's day - 1976. Diane, Wiggy and Paul Keeble.

Robert and Priscilla Savage and their family, c. 1920.

William French, c. 1850. We think this is probably the earliest photograph in the archive.

Henry Puttock and Lizzie Puttock.

Mariah (left) and Charlotte Poacher.

Daisy Bell Cooper (née Stebbing) aged 15 in 1908.

William Woolnough 30 July 1919

Dick French in his World War I uniform.

Elizabeth Ann Rose (née Brightwell)

RIGHT: Molecatcher James Sparrowhawk 'Hawky' Smith in front of Blaxhall Church. Date probably early 1880s.

IRO K681/1/44/8

Clayton Keeble

Albert and Agnes Clark c.1930

Alice Ling

Maud Gissing and Clara Hewitt, who were sisters.

George Poacher aged 17 in 1941

Susan French and Caroline Price outside the 'old' Cherry Tree Cottage, Stone Common.

Alice Poacher in front of 1 and 2 Stone Cottages Stone Common

Kate and George Messenger outside the bungalow 'Windrift'.

Dick 'Biff' Smy worked at Fir Tree Farm and lived at Stone Common for a number of years.

Harry Cable Snr and Harry Cable Jnr

Arthur Hewitt

Walter Hammond with Old Barn Cottages behind.

Maude Keeble

Will Ling and his son Derek Ling

Ivy Keeble

Edna Smith 1937

Grace Scotchmer, Javey Pryke, Hilda
Pryke, May Pryke holding Peter Anthony
with Christine Pryke in the front.

Special Policeman Arthur Smith c.1941

Bob Ling, Ronnie Ling and Wilfred Ling

Mary French in her back garden with Ship Cottages in the background.

'Seed' George Bennett

Frank Woolnough at the top of School Hill, 1983.

Ernie Ling

Fred Buoy

ABOVE Back left: Sheila Scopes (née Shaw), Susan French, Mollie Pictor (née Mayhew), Mary Mayhew, Mary French, Dick French. Sitting left: Marian Burch, Dorothy Double (née French), Mrs Double, Florrie Shaw holding Diane Ling whose christening was the reason for the celebration. Front left : David Double and Robert Burch, right.

Peter and Iris Fletcher on their 25th Wedding anniversary, 1975.

From left: Jimmy Knights, Ena Plant, Tommy Curtis and Alice Woolnough on Heath Walk.

Left to right: Frank Shaw, Florrie Shaw, Mary Mayhew and Fred Mayhew

The Sunshine Club of Blaxhall.

Shirley (née Hewitt) and John Taylor at his surprise 50th birthday celebration.

From left: Kenny French, David Savage, 'Tedder' French, Geoff Ling, Alfie Ling and Julie Ferguson with her dogs.

Derek Keeble practising the Last Post.

Sarah Maud Skeet and Walter Skeet leaning over their garden fence chatting to their neighbour Jenny Webb.

Jim Grubbs, recent landlord of The Ship Inn, Blaxhall.

Kenny Keeble on the way to his common yard on Stone Common.

Robin Graham.

Tilly and Tim Locker outside of Sandlands, Mill Common.

Paul Keeble and his son William.

**These photographs were taken by the late Chris Long for the Blaxhall Archive Group exhibition in May 2005.**

Rona and Nobby Lear at Old Foss Cottage with Jenks.

George and Joyce Phillips, Stone Common.

Pauline Alibaster.

Deborah Mawson at Holly Tree, School Road.

Jeff and Tonya in front of Waterloo House.

Jill and Nigel at Vine Cottage, Church Road.

Kath and Ray Poacher at 'Poacher's Rest', Station Road.

The Reverend Nigella Youngs-Dunnett (right) and Joyce Phillips at the crafts display during the Blaxhall Festival 2004.

Peter and Janet Long with foster sons Shaun Baxter (left front) and Martin Stewart at Glebe Farm.

Dorothy Keeble at Keeble's Yard, Hilly Fields.

Maggie Grenham and Rod West at Flint Cottage, Stone Common.

Clara Jenkins out and about around the village collecting for the Red Cross.

Chris and Amanda Long with Amani at the Coach house.

Daphne and John Gant with 'Barney' the driving pony at Old Barn Cottages.

June and Richard Rope at Grove Farm.

Diane and Roger Miles with son Freddy and pony at Old Barn Cottages.

Doris Dunne getting it done at Rose Cottage, Mill Common.

Molly Pictor at home at Greenbanks, Stone Common.

Jacquie and David Pugh at Gorse Farm with James and Emma and spaniels Barney and Rubble.

Joy Shaw with her flock of sheep.

Phylli and Les Heard, Bramble Cottage, Stone Common.

From left: Karen Lear, Susie Watling and Jamie Cutts working on his common yard at Mill Common. *Not a Chris Long photograph.*

# REFERENCES

## Introduction. The Time Before This

[1] Evans, G.E., *Ask the Fellows who Cut the Hay*, Faber & Faber

## Chapter One. People and Places

[1] The 1674 Hearth Tax Returns. The Green Books
[2] Blaxhall Commons by T. Cole IRO HA49/C2/7/1
[3] Blaxhall Settlement Orders IRO FC 133/G5/1-29
[4] Kenney, A c.1930 Notes on Suffolk Windmills
[5] Flint, B. *Suffolk Windmills*
[6] Evans, G.E., *The Farm and the Village*, Faber & Faber
[7] Coroner's Inquest HB10:50/20

## Chapter Two. Farming the Land

[1] War Agriculture Executive Committee  WWII Farm Surveys  P.R.O. Kew

## Chapter Five. St. Peter's Hidden Keys

[1] Coroner's Inquest Index 1767 - 1858
[2] Blatchley, J. and Northeast, P.  2006 *Decoding Flint Flushwork*  Ipswich
[3] Davey, D.E. Miscellaneous collections. B.L. Add. Mss. 19,185 - 19,197
[4] Visitations of the Archdeacon of the diocese  FAA/6/17
[5] Dymond, D. 1990 *A lost social institution: The Camping Close*  Rural History 1,2:165-192

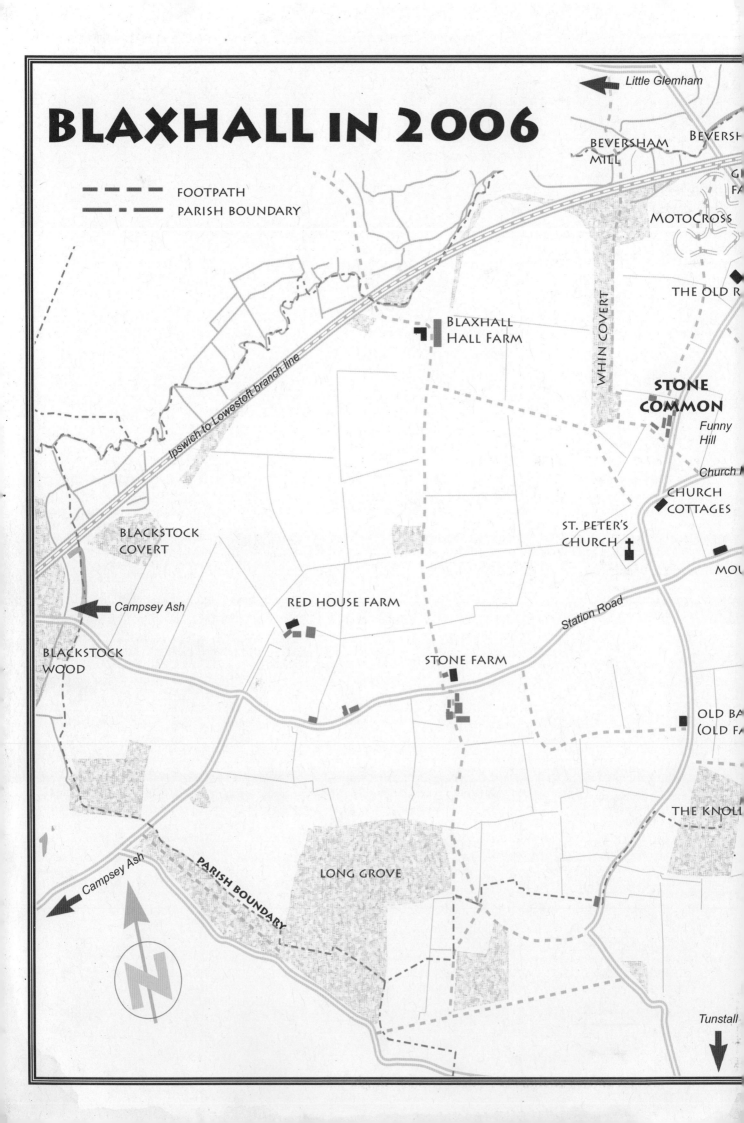